LINGUISTICS

in Proper Perspective

Second Edition

Pose Lamb

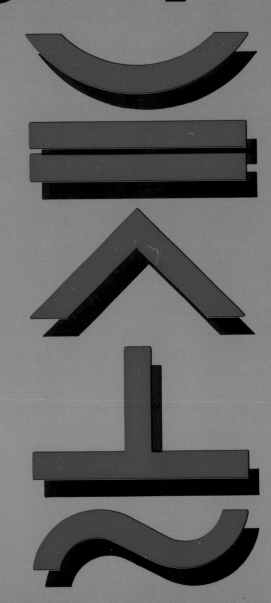

Linguistics in Proper Perspective

Second Edition

Merrill's

INTERNATIONAL SERIES
IN EDUCATION

Under the Editorship of
Kimball Wiles
University of Florida

Linguistics in Proper Perspective

Second Edition

Pose Lamb

Purdue University

Charles E. Merrill Publishing Company
A Bell & Howell Company
Columbus, Ohio

Published by
Charles E. Merrill Publishing Company
A Bell & Howell Company
Columbus, Ohio 43216

The book was set in Times Roman.
The Production Editor was Linda Hillis.
The cover was designed by Will Chenoweth.

International Standard Book Number: 0-675-08596-9
Library of Congress Catalog Card Number: 76-40572
1 2 3 4 5 6 7—82 81 80 79 78 77

Printed in the United States of America

Preface

There have been significant developments in the field of linguistics since the first edition of *Linguistics in Proper Perspective* was published. It is clearly time to report new research evidence, to review and react to new concepts, and to acquaint classroom teachers with the ideas of those who are currently most active in the field. The purpose of this edition is the same as the purpose of the first, to provide pre-service and in-service elementary teachers with some of the findings of linguists and to discuss the implications of these findings for teaching reading, spelling, and grammar.

To aid in understanding some of the complex ideas, concepts, and generalizations proposed by linguists, it seems appropriate to present to elementary educators a brief overview of the field and discuss some major linguistic principles for classroom application. These principles may be succinctly stated as follows:

1. Spoken language is older than any writing system. Even at this point in time, the majority of the world's languages have not been written. Without denying the importance of our writing systems, it is probably true that speech communicates more effectively and that gestures and facial expressions do more than commas and semicolons to convey meaning (or disguise it!).
2. Language changes—because it is arbitrary and created by people. The human race is not the servant of language; rather, language changes when new ideas, products, and institutions cause people to recognize the need for such change.

Change in language is not rapid; much of the English spoken in Chaucer's day can be understood today.

3. One language is not superior to another. Even languages which have not been written have conventions of structure, in sound and in grammar, which can be scientifically studied. Although these conventions have certain elements in common, it is unwise to attempt to transfer these from one language to another.

4. Although our language, American English, does *not* have a built in system of standards to tell us what is right and wrong, it is appropriate to speak of standard and nonstandard usage. The standards developed represent patterns of usage which are acceptable among the educated people of a community, and these vary from community to community and from generation to generation. The term *nonstandard* should *not* be construed as suggesting that the grammars referred to are without system or organization. Nevertheless, standard grammars are more acceptable to most speakers of standard grammars, and the use of a nonstandard usage *may,* and frequently does, result in penalties of an academic, professional, and, perhaps, even personal nature.

In the chapters which follow, these principles are amplified and discussed in such a way that the elementary teachers' work in the areas of reading, spelling, and grammar might be enriched and appropriate linguistic concepts incorporated into their teaching. The carefully selected lists of references at the end of each chapter add depth and provide additional data in areas in which the reader may have a special interest or recognize a specific deficiency.

Contents

terials of a More Traditional Nature, *43*. Implications for Today's and Tomorrow's Reading Programs, *45*. Phonics and Linguistics, *47*. Elementary Teachers and Knowledge of Their Language, *47*. Summary, *47*.

1

Linguistics and Language Arts

Elementary teachers continue to receive persistent and repeated advice, even pleas, to base their teaching of the language arts[1] on a solid "linguistic" basis. Textbooks, films, programmed materials, and media of every type are being produced to aid the teachers of children from kindergarten through sixth grade in making the difficult transition from "traditional, old-fashioned" techniques to more modern methods of language teaching. *Linguistics* is a term which can no longer be avoided or ignored.

Importance of Linguistic Knowledge for Elementary Teachers

Although he may be confused and bewildered by the profusion of articles, books, and revised teaching materials purported to have a linguistic basis, the elementary teacher is usually eager to utilize the results of research in the language arts and to make appropriate adjustments in his teaching. However, when he attempts to investigate the field of linguistic knowledge as it applies to teaching in the elementary schools, too often he finds disagreement, confusion, and contradictory advice instead of enlightenment and help. Knowledge concerning all facets of the structure of our

---

1. The language arts are here defined as those areas of the elementary school curriculum which deal with listening, speaking, reading, and writing.

language is expanding quite rapidly, and it is difficult indeed to know which "new" theories or concepts to accept and which to reject.

Why should the teacher enter this "jungle" then? Why not wait until guidelines are clearer, until the teacher is more certain of what he knows and doesn't know? Because, in the first place, materials are being produced at an increasingly rapid rate, and elementary teachers must decide which materials to use, how much linguistic emphasis to incorporate into their spelling and reading programs, and which linguistic approach seems most appropriate. There is at least one other important reason for making the effort to understand linguistics and its implications for elementary teaching. A few widely used teaching techniques (emphasis on isolated sound-symbol relationships in phonics instruction, for example, or diagramming sentences as part of instruction in grammar) are *clearly* outdated. One need not be a linguist on the "growing edge" of his field of competence to adapt and make full use of some basic linguistic principles. The proliferation of terminology (allophones, phonemes, graphemes) and disagreements about the most useful approach to grammar (transformational or structural) are of major concern to graduate students majoring in linguistics and to advanced scholars in the field, of course, but at the level of elementary school classroom practice, the areas of agreement outnumber and outweigh in importance the areas of greatest controversy among linguists.

This book represents an effort to discuss, in general terms, the work of linguists as they attempt to learn more about our language; its origins, its structure, and its sounds. More specifically, an effort has been made to indicate possible and useful applications of linguistics, as a field of knowledge, a discipline, pursued by respected scholar-scientists, to language arts programs in elementary school classrooms. Oversimplification is a pitfall in any effort of this type. This is especially true in writing about a field that is expanding and changing as rapidly as the field of linguistics. Unfortunately, only a few linguists have tried to explain their work so the typical classroom teacher could understand it and make curricular or methodological changes and adaptations in terms of the new knowledge. It is the well-known problem of the theorists versus the practitioners. In trying to relate basic elements of linguistic theory to classroom practice, undoubtedly some important understandings will be overlooked or developed in a less thorough manner than might be desirable. If, at times, the vocabulary in this book seems too nontechnical, too simple to express significant and complex concepts adequately, the reader should keep in mind that the anticipated audience for this book is not the linguist, working with tape recorder and computer, familiar with Pike, Chomsky, and other scholars, but elementary school teachers whose problems relate to *how* and *how much* to teach as well as *what* to teach in the field of language arts.

Definition of Terms

The terminology problem, the difficulty of interpreting correctly certain terms encountered in reading about linguistics, is significant enough to justify the inclusion of a glossary at the end of this book. It is hoped that the reader will find this useful in reading not only this book but also other linguistic material. However, one cannot really proceed any further without defining two of the most basic terms: *linguist* and *linguistics.*

A *linguist,* in essence, is a student of human languages, a scholar-scientist whose field of competence is human language. A linguist may or may not be proficient in speaking and/or writing a variety of languages. It is what he knows of the basic processes of the languages he studies—their structures or grammars and their sounds—which is significant. One can speak and write in several languages (and many do) without deserving the title of linguist. The linguist's work is primarily that of understanding and describing the nature of *human* language, including its functioning processes. The use of "functioning" inaccurately suggests that perhaps a linguist has little or no interest in the historical development of languages. One type of linguist, called a historical linguist, deals almost entirely with tracing the origins of words and various types of sentence patterns, and studies the development of dialects and languages. All linguists have some interest in the changes that have occurred in languages, and one of the basic and most generally accepted linguistic principles is that languages change and that such change is healthy, normal, and not to be deplored.

Linguistics, it would logically follow, is clearly and briefly defined as the scientific study of language. Such study may concentrate on the sounds of language (phonology), the origin and changing meaning of words (etymology and semantics), or the arrangements of words in a meaningful context (syntax).

The Structure of Language

Language is another term which probably should be defined at this point. Girsdansky's definition is a very useful one: "Language is a set of arbitrary symbols (words) which are placed in orderly relationship with one another according to conventions accepted and understood by the speakers, for the transmission of messages."[2]

Noam Chomsky and Morris Halle take a somewhat different viewpoint. They write: "We may think of a language as a set of sentences, each with an ideal phonetic form and an associated intrinsic semantic interpretation. The grammar of the language is the system of rules that specifies this sound-meaning correspondence."[3]

The Development of American English—
An Overview

Humans probably developed the ability to communicate with each other through sounds and combinations of sounds soon after their evolution, or arrival on earth, as thinking, purposive, upright mammals. There are a number of interesting theories concerning the manner in which this ability to communicate developed. The "pooh-

---

2. Michael Girsdansky, *The Adventure of Language* (Englewood Cliffs, N.J.: Prentice-Hall, 1963), p. 3.

3. Noam Chomsky and Morris Halle, *The Sound Pattern of English* (New York: Harper & Row, 1968), p. 3.

pooh" theory holds that language evolved from early exclamations of fear and surprise; the "bow-wow" theory holds that language developed from human attempts to imitate natural sounds, animal sounds among others.

After reviewing these and several other theories of the origin of language, West concludes:

> So, by recalling the past and planning for the future, man advanced to time binding. His mind broke through the sense limiting medium of time and he was now able to hold the continuum of time—present, past, and future, simultaneously in his mind through word-symbols. To expand his new world of objects, events, space, time, and qualities such as mass, velocity, form, color, texture, he created yet more word-symbols. With more ideas to think about and discuss with his companions, he increased his inventory of word-symbols, originally indicators of concrete phenomena that he could see close at hand, to include more abstract symbols. . . . Such words in turn allowed even more abstractions of thought. Society became more complex, and so did language. Thus cause became effect and effect became cause.[4]

But, again, we have no definite historical evidence to actually show the progression from a primitive language to a sophisticated one.

Latin and Greek Influences on the
English Language

Dineen provides an acceptable answer to the question, Why bother with even a brief reference to languages which have such limited relevance to American English as it is spoken and written today?

> One reason for studying the ancient and medieval work on language has already been mentioned: its outlook is the point of view basic to traditional grammar, much of which makes sense only when we put it into such a framework. A structural reason for such study is that we cannot freely know what something is until we know what it is not . . . much of the work of the ancients had rigor and consistency, which accounts for their satisfaction with the answers they obtained.[5]

Language Study—Greek. Greek Sophists recommended the use of the sentences in which phrases and clauses would be of precisely equal length, and they developed a technical vocabulary of rhetoric which, translated of course, is still used today.

Plato's interest in language was based on his belief that one could learn about things by studying their names and the acceptable or conventional combinations of terms dealing with these things. According to Dineen, "he did not investigate the arbitrary, conventional system of language."[6] In contrast, Aristotle was concerned

---

4. Fred West, *The Way of Language* (New York: Harcourt Brace Jovanovich, 1975), pp. 14–15.

5. Francis Dineen, *An Introduction to General Linguistics* (New York: Holt, Rinehart & Winston, 1967), p. 72.

6. Ibid., p. 79.

with language and language facts. He made clear distinctions between word and sentence forms, speaking and writing styles, and word meanings, alone and in context. Stoics took issue with Aristotle and held that there was a connection between the sounds of a language and the things they represented. Neither Plato nor Aristotle was particularly concerned with analyzing the morphological facets of their languages, nor were the Stoics.

Traditional grammarians, even today, discuss the languages with which they're working in terms of categories developed by Dionysius Thrax, whose *Grammar* has had tremendous impact upon students of language.[7]

Language Study—Latin. Priscian provides the most thorough and authoritative description of his native language, Latin. His work, a set of eighteen books, also provides a model still utilized by traditional grammarians. For example, he is responsible for isolating and defining eight parts of speech, and these still have general acceptability among members of this traditionalist group. Dineen notes that Priscian's work can be criticized for his lack of emphasis on morphology and for his failure to define *meaning,* although this concept was central to much of his theory.

The Latin and Greek languages had much in common. Gleason comments: "The Greek terminology was translated rather literally, ultimately to be adapted from Latin to English and to most other languages of Europe."[8] He adds:

Following the Renaissance, the newer languages of Europe gradually established themselves as vehicles for literature and later for science. Latin, however, remained central in the education of all scholars. The grammarians and rhetoricians only very slowly shifted their attention to the vernaculars. The first treatments of other languages began to appear in the fifteenth century but it was much later before they became of great importance. The first English grammars appeared in the sixteenth century and became influential only in the eighteenth.[9]

Until the nineteenth century, Latin remained as the central subject in the curriculum, and interest in the study of languages other than Latin was slow to develop. The rebirth of interest in Greek and Hebrew (also in the nineteenth century) had a similar effect. Nevertheless, traditional grammarians still rely heavily on analyses developed, and most appropriate, for Latin, not American English, except for purposes of historical interest; noting where language study *has* been in order to have a more adequate concept of where it *is* and to assess probable future developments in the field.

English belongs to the Germanic branch of the language family called either Indo-European or Aryan. This family includes the Romance languages (French, Spanish, Italian), Slavonic languages (Polish, Czechoslovakian, and Russian), the Germanic languages (Dutch, "High" and "Low" German, Swedish, Norwegian, Danish, and, of course, English), as well as several other language groups.

---

7. R. H. Robins, *Dionysius Thrax and the Western Grammatical Tradition* (London: Philological Society, 1957), pp. 67–106.

8. Dineen, *Introduction to General Linguistics,* pp. 118–20.

9. Henry Gleason, *Linguistics and English Grammar* (New York: Holt, Rinehart & Winston, 1965), p. 29.

The Latin language came to Great Britain with the Roman troops of the Emperor Claudius (about A.D. 50), and its influence was felt as long as the influence of Rome itself. However, the Roman Empire declined in influence and the Celts, Britain's original inhabitants, were unable to withstand the onslaughts of new and somewhat less civilized conquerors.

Old English

German tribes invaded and settled in Great Britain, probably early in the fifth century A.D., and this is recognized as one of the most important and significant events in the development of the English language. The German language eventually became English as we know it today. The historian Bede writes that these tribes were the Angles, who gave their name to the nation which finally evolved (Angle-land, Angleland, and, finally, England); the Saxons (the largest, in terms of numbers, of the tribes); and the Jutes. The language they found established was a combination of Celtic, spoken in the country, and Latin, a holdover from several Roman invasions, spoken in the cities and towns. The language of the inhabitants had little influence on the conquerors, for

> it could never be fashionable for them to show an acquaintance with that despised tongue by using now and then a Celtic word. On the other hand, the Celt would have to learn the language of his masters and learn it well; he could not think of addressing his superiors in his own unintelligible gibberish, and if the first generation did not learn good English, the second and third would, while the influence they themselves exercised on English would be infinitesimal.[10]

Considering the Christianization of Britain about A.D. 600 and the resulting increased status of Latin, the language of the church, it is remarkable that English showed so little Latin influence, during this period at least. Most of the words added were, of course, those of a religious nature. Jesperson notes that "the Old English Language, as we have seen, was essentially self sufficing; its foreign elements were few and did not modify the character of the language as a whole."[11]

The next hallmark in the development of the English language was the Danish invasion of Britain about A.D. 800. The two languages, it will be recalled, came from similar roots, and the influence of the conqueror on the conquered was less than might have been anticipated; the two groups already had much in common, linguistically speaking. A few new words—*die, they, them, their, happy, anger*—were added to the English vocabulary.

Middle English

The date 1066, which marks William the Conqueror's victory in the Battle of Hastings, is usually identified as the beginning of French influence on the English language. This influence lasted for well over two hundred years and added much additional vocabulary to the English language.

---

10. Otto Jesperson, *Growth and Structure of the English Language* (New York: Macmillan Co., 1938), p. 40.
11. Ibid., p. 61.

It is difficult to overestimate the influence of the French conquerors on the English language. Speakers of English came to feel that French was a more fully developed language with a more mature and sophisticated literature and with a superior "linguistic status." French was the language of the upper classes, the rulers. Sir Walter Scott notes, in *Ivanhoe,* that several animals with English names (cow, sheep, swine) assume French names when they appear on the dinner table (beef, mutton, pork).

The Renaissance also left its mark upon Great Britain, and the English language as well, partly because of the fact that the Norman French had already pretty well broken Anglo-Saxon resistance to "linguistic change." Latin grammar became the only respectable grammar, although it did not fit the English language, then or now.

What might be called the second period of Latin influence, beginning in the fourteenth century, continued throughout the Middle English period and is, of course, felt today in "Modern English." A few linguists are prone to consider the Latin influence unfortunate, perhaps feeling that English would have been a stronger language, and a purer one, if it had not been so compromised by its Latin ancestors. We cannot deny, however, that we owe a great debt to the Latin language. Much of the richness of our language and a great deal of its vocabulary (about one word in five, and each scientific advance seems to add more) are the direct results of Latin influence.

Modern English

This period is usually thought of as beginning about A.D. 1500, and it can be said that the language we speak today belongs in this period, although there are striking differences between current, "modern" English and Shakespeare's English.

The most significant characteristic of our language is its flexibility. It changes, grows, and adapts as the need for such adjustment is indicated. It is an important language. As Pei suggests (perhaps in an overstatement):

> English is, at present, the most widely studied language in countries where it is not native, being the favored foreign language in the higher education curriculums of such widely scattered nations as Russia, Japan and Turkey. It is conspicuously the language of trade and business transactions, and bids fair to become a tongue of common intercourse in many parts of the world. Three-fourths of the world's newspapers are printed in English. English is the language of over three-fifths of the world's radio stations. It has a literature as flourishing as any, and has recently become one of the leading tongues of international scholarship and scientific research. More than half of the world's scientific and technical periodicals are printed entirely or partly in English.[12]

Linguistics as a Field of Study

Some contributions of students of Latin and Greek have already been noted. In this section, attention will be devoted to those linguists whose contributions to our knowledge of American English have perhaps been more direct.

---

12. From *The Story of Language* by Mario Pei. Copyright © 1965, 1949 by Mario Pei. Published by J. B. Lippincott Co. (Mentor edition, p. 247.)

Linguistic Study: From Rask to Bloomfield

The linguist Erasmus Rask presented a paper before the Danish Academy of Science in 1814 in which he stressed the importance of studying the total structure of a language, not studying it in bits and pieces. This appears to be a consistent aim or objective of linguists, for modern linguists state the same objective.

It may surprise the reader to learn that Jakob Grimm, one of the editors and compilers of *Grimm's Fairy Tales,* was a serious and scientific student of language. His *Deutsche Grammatik* (German Grammar) was published in 1822.[13] His chief contribution involved publicizing a governing principle for a complex of phonetic changes in language originally formulated by Rask. August Schleicher (1821–1863) was keenly interested in vocabulary and also in charting relationships among languages. To Schleicher also goes the credit for establishing the principle that language does not decay, but changes, and that such change is normal and is to be expected.

Fries identifies the publication of two books by William Whitney, in 1867[14] and 1875,[15] as the next events of significance in the field of linguistics. He writes:

> Before 1818, questions concerning language—of origin, of diversity, of relationship, of structure, of meaning—were approached primarily through speculation and appeals to authority. The fifty years from the linguistic ground-breaking of Rask and Grimm to the publication of Whitney's books saw the development of a considerable body of verifiable knowledge concerning language, built up through the use of techniques accessible to all who would become proficient workers in linguistics.[16]

The first fifty years of the scientific study of language produced the following principles, generally accepted by students of language in the second half of the twentieth century:

1. Languages change, and the changes that occur are not haphazard or accidental. They can be mapped and charted. This principle was accepted only after a great deal of controversy, and not until after 1875.
2. The changes that occur are not indicative of decay or degeneration; rather, they are hallmarks of a living, growing, healthy organism.
3. It is not the task of a linguist to *prescribe* correct usage; he *describes* a language as it is and as it is used by educated speakers and writers.

A theory of Ferdinand de Saussure (1857–1913) might be listed as a fourth principle—language is arbitrary. Language serves as a link between thought and sound; when the band, or link, between the encoder and that which is encoded changes, the language changes.

---

13. Charles Fries, *Linguistics and Reading* (New York: Holt, Rinehart & Winston. Copyright © 1962, 1963 by Charles Fries), p. 37.
14. William Whitney, *Language and the Study of Language: Twelve Lectures on the Principles of Linguistic Science* (New York: Charles Scribner's Sons, 1867).
15. William Whitney, *The Life and Growth of Language: An Outline of Linguistic Science* (New York: Charles Scribner's Sons, 1875).
16. Fries, *Linguistics and Reading,* p. 40.

From the "Prague School," whose members were direct intellectual descendants of de Saussure, we get the concept of the *phoneme* (usually defined as the smallest significant unit of sound) and the approach to linguistic study called *phonology* (the study of the function of speech sound). The concept of the phoneme is not a simple one. There is little agreement about the number of phonemes in the English language; it is variously stated that there are thirty-five, thirty-eight, forty-four, or—according to some more cautious writers—from thirty-five to forty-seven. The confusion exists partly as a result of the several levels of interpretation of the word *significant*. A sound which is significant in one dialect, one which truly reflects a meaning shift (zip–sip), may be less significant in another dialect. The definition of the phoneme also varies with the "school" of linguistics to which one belongs; Noam Chomsky rejects completely the definition of a phoneme given above. It is a definition that satisfies most linguists, however.

This condensed overview of linguistics would not be complete without discussing the contributions of Franz Boas (1858–1942), Edmund Sapir (1884–1939), and Leonard Bloomfield (1887–1948) to the field of linguistics as we know it today.

Linguistic Study: From Bloomfield to Chomsky

Boas and Sapir were anthropologists who developed a strong interest in studying language. They also contributed a great deal to the field of descriptive analysis of language. Nevertheless, the most significant fact about their work was that it served as a solid foundation for Bloomfield's work, and today Bloomfield's work is more widely known by linguists and the public than that of either of the men whose work he studied so carefully. Bloomfield's major contribution was his book, *Language,* which has become a classic. The year in which *Language* was published, 1933, is a modern landmark in the field of scientific language study. Bloomfield advocated the study of language through structural analysis, *independent of a study of semantics or meaning.* He wrote: "The statement of meaning is therefore a weak point in language study, and will remain so until human knowledge is very far beyond its present state. In practice, we define the meaning of a linguistic form, wherever we can, in terms of some other science."[17] For example, the definition of a verb as "an action word" is of little use, Bloomfield would contend, because it tells us nothing of a verb's grammatical function.

The field of linguistics is a very active one; otherwise there would be no purpose for a book of this type. Kenneth Pike, Zellig Harris, George Trager, Noam Chomsky, and Bernard Bloch are just a few linguists who have made recent contributions to linguistic knowledge.

Pike has developed a very useful guide for writing unfamiliar and previously unwritten languages—a phonetic alphabet, similar to the International Phonetic Alphabet (IPA), but with a few striking differences. Pike's alphabet, and another phonetic alphabet developed by George Trager and Henry Lee Smith, include nine different representations for vowel sounds in English; the IPA lists thirteen. (It should be noted that the IPA was developed to represent the sounds of many lan-

---

17. Leonard Bloomfield, *Language* (New York: Holt, Rinehart & Winston, 1933), p. 139.

guages, not English alone.) Harris has studied not only phonemes, words, or sentences, but portions of discourse larger than a sentence. He writes: "The successive sentences of a connected discourse . . . offer fertile soil for the methods of descriptive linguistics, since these methods study the relative distribution of elements within a connected stretch of speech."[18]

Harris has expanded the notion that sentences make words; he would add that groups of sentences make words, or words achieve their primary significance when studied in the context of a sentence or a paragraph. Harris has worked in the field of transformational grammar, which differs rather strikingly from the decomposition-by-sentence-parsing approach with which the reader is probably quite familiar. Transformational grammar appears to rest on the basic assumption that all the sentences of a language are either kernel sentences or transformations of kernel sentences. The number of kernels possible or acceptable in a given language is finite or limited. It is through transformation of these kernels that we gain the infinite variety of sentences we have in English. Harris writes:

> Our picture of a language then, includes a finite number of actual kernel sentences, all cast in a small number of sentence structures built out of a few morpheme classes by means of a few constructional rules; a set of combining and introducing elements; and a set of elementary transformations such that one or more transformations may be applied to any kernel sentence or group of kernel sentences, and such that any properly transformed sentences may be added sequentially by means of combiners.[19]

Transformational grammar will be dealt with in greater detail in chapter 4, "Linguistics and the Teaching of Grammar and Usage."

Another post-Bloomfield contribution was the concept of the *juncture*. The significance of juncture, or pause, is illustrated by the difference in meaning conveyed by placing juncture in these utterances in different positions:

1. a name
2. an aim

Obviously, differences in *pitch* also play a part in making combinations of the same "words" into quite different kinds of utterances. The meaning in the following utterance is altered significantly by changes in pitch:

1. What are we having for breakfast, mother? (Rising pitch on *mother*)
2. What are we having for breakfast, mother? (Falling pitch on *mother*)

Modern structural linguists have identified four levels of pitch and an equal number of stress levels.

---

18. Zellig Harris, "Discourse Analysis," *Language* 28 (1952): 19.
19. Zellig Harris, "Co-occurrence and Transformation in Linguistic Structure," *Language* 33 (1957): 399.

The reader might try reading aloud the following utterance, placing the stress on the italicized words, to gain some idea of the role of stress in conveying meaning:

Are *you* going to eat that food?
Are you going to *eat* that food?
Are you going to eat *that* food?
Are you going to eat that *food?*

Variations in levels of stress become apparent as each utterance is read. *Eat* in each of the sentences probably received more stress than *are,* regardless of the word receiving the most stress. Stress variation is an aid in conveying meaning in a given utterance and helps to differentiate meaning variations in similar utterances.

Change in patterns of pitch can elicit different responses from the decoder of a linguistic message—the listener. Using the suggested pitch patterns following each utterance (highest pitch is indicated by the numeral three, the lowest by the numeral one), read the utterances aloud and note the difference in meaning:

He's a good teacher.   (2-3-2-1)
He's a good teacher.   (2-2-3-2)

Most would suspect that the second utterance was something less than a compliment, suggesting that the ability to teach was the man's *only* skill or area of competence! Pitch, stress, and pause, or juncture, may be labeled *suprasegmental phonemes,* and structural linguists have helped all those who are interested in language, and how it is learned and used, to become aware of the impact of these suprasegmental phonemes on meaning.

Everyone is aware of the role of the lifted eyebrow, the nod, or the frown in supporting or refuting the meaning of the speaker's words. Linguists have determined that these are not instinctive, but are learned, acquired, and arbitrary, much as the vocabulary and syntax of a language are. Japanese people respond to an embarrassing or frustrating situation with something that sounds like our giggle; it is actually quite unlike our use of this form of laughter, and this difference is important in communicating between representatives of the two cultures. The patterned bodily movements that accompany speech (excluding formal gestures, for the most part) are often termed *kinesis.*

Finally, it might be noted that, in recounting the contributions of modern linguists, the contribution of Noam Chomsky deserves some discussion. Chomsky calls his grammar "generative grammar"; he writes:

A generative grammar is a system of explicit rules that assign to each sequence of phones (sounds[20]), whether of the observed corpus (text-sentence, paragraph, etc.) or not, a structural description that contains all information about how this sequence of phones is a properly formed or grammatical sentence, and if not,

---

20. Words in parentheses not in original text.

in what respects it deviates from well-formedness. In particular, then, this grammar distinguishes a class of perfectly well formed (fully grammatical) sentences.[21]

It may be of some comfort to the elementary teacher struggling with these sophisticated theories to know that linguists disagree among themselves. The existence of three such widely different grammatical theories as structural, transformational-generative, and case grammar is adequate testimony to this disagreement. Many questions remain to be answered before one of these theories gains universal acceptance, and before that happens still other theories may be proposed. It should not be disturbing to find so many competing linguistic theories. This is the hallmark of a living, vigorous, and growing science. Within the next few years, additional knowledge will enable linguists, and those who teach children something of the nature of their language, to determine which approach or combination of approaches has the most merit, and which is (or are) the most fruitful for instructional as well as research purposes. Materials have been and are currently being developed to help the elementary teacher make some needed changes in his approach to grammar and usage.

Developments in the field of linguistics during the period since 1925 might be summarized as follows:

1. This was the period during which the phoneme was conceptualized, although linguists are still arguing about the value and the significance of the phoneme and disagree when asked to state a given numeral as representing the number of significant speech sounds in American English.

2. Thanks particularly to the work of Bloomfield, *meaning* assumed a different role in language study. It was Bloomfield who insisted that language should be studied through analysis of its structure, rather than through a study of semantics or meaning.

3. Some linguists have focused on analysis of large units of language, *discourse analysis,* feeling that even the sentence was somewhat too small a unit to give a useful description of linguistic structures.

4. Levels of pitch and stress (four of each have been identified) and the concept of juncture have aided the linguist in his search for a more complete description of a language. Juncture refers to the pauses or near-pauses that connect various parts of a sentence. Stress refers to changes in a speaker's volume; pitch, to the highness or lowness of a sound, the frequency of the vibrations of sound waves reaching the listener's ear. Pitch, stress, and juncture have a profound impact upon the rhythm of a given language and its phonology, and illustrations were included in this chapter suggesting the impact of stress, pitch, and juncture on the meaning of an utterance. Pitch, stress, and juncture have been collectively labeled suprasegmental phonemes, impositions upon the sound units of language that give added meaning to the utterance.

5. Kinesis, supporting or refuting the meaning conveyed by a group of sounds through facial expression, smiles, and so forth, has been studied by linguists

21. Noam Chomsky, "Some Methodological Remarks on Generative Grammar," *Word* 17 (1961): 221.

during the period being summarized here. One significant discovery is that these nonlanguage aspects of language are arbitrary and are learned, just as vocabulary and syntax are learned.

6. Linguists have made full use of appropriate technological advances—the tape recorder and the computer, for example—and, as a result, languages can now be described with much more precision than ever before.

7. Finally, a few linguists, although perhaps not enough, have become interested in sharing their findings with classroom teachers. Particularly in the fields of reading and spelling, as well as in the field of grammar, elementary school teachers have benefited.

Language Acquisition and Development

Professional literature has too often included the misinformation that language development is relatively complete by the time a child reaches the age of four or five. Presumably, this statement is designed to preclude the underestimation of children's language skills by kindergarten and first grade teachers. Four and five year olds do indeed know a great deal about their language, and "normal" children of four and five use words and sentences with a great deal of facility. However, even a cursory comparison of the linguistic sophistication of a five and a ten year old is adequate evidence that change, growth, and development are still occurring during this period. Knowledge regarding the areas in which growth and development are to be expected is of obvious value to the elementary language arts teacher and should be fundamental to the programs developed for children and preadolescents. Wanat's question is pertinent:

"What is language development and why bother about it?"[22] The study of language development (also referred to as developmental psycholinguistics, developmental linguistics, or the study of language acquisition) tries to account for how the "meaningless" cooing, gurgling, and babbling sounds of the infant turn into the meaningful language spoken by the adult.

Noam Chomsky claims that language acquisition is a process in which the child formulates a theory (description) of his language. It is as if the child were a linguist writing a new grammar, but Chomsky notes that the child is probably not even conscious of the rules he formulates. "Some of the skills which underlie language development are: the mental ability to deal with the world, the ability to remember things, the ability to break down the language one hears into units of meaning and recombine these units, and the ability to generalize."[23]

Psycholinguists have devoted considerable attention to the role of imitation in language acquisition and development. There is no question that some sounds, even syntactical structures, are learned this way. However, it is also clear that children use many expressions which they have rarely, if ever, heard an adult use. Further, and teachers are perhaps even more keenly aware of this than parents, children's

22. Stanley Wanat, "Language Acquisition: Basic Issues," *The Reading Teacher* 25 (1971): 142.

23. Ibid., p. 143.

language is *highly* resistant to change through adult intervention. Without entirely discounting the role of imitation and the value of rewards for achievement from significant adults, the position is taken that more than these factors is involved in the acquisition and development of language.

Language is difficult to suppress in a human being. Acquisition and development are likely to occur despite tremendous physical, intellectual, and social obstacles. It also seems increasingly clear that this development occurs in a sequence which varies little, even across cultures. For example, infants utter vowel sounds before consonant sounds, and children's vocabularies consist of nouns, verbs, and adjectives before function words (determiners, prepositions, and conjunctions) are added. Of course, the rate of progress through these sequences varies greatly from person to person.

Akmajian and Heny reflect what is probably the most currently acceptable viewpoint on language learning:

> Children learn language by constructing their own grammars (i.e., sets of internalized rules) and they do this by a process of analysis: constructing, testing, and modifying hypotheses about the sentences they encounter. At first, these hypotheses amount to guesses about the nature of the rules that underlie the sentences of the language. The rules are incorporated into the child's developing grammar, which in time more and more closely approximates the grammars of the adult speech community.[24]

Language Development During the Elementary School Years

Although such divisions are arbitrary, and may contribute to a point of view toward language which is particularized rather than integrated, it is, perhaps, useful to discuss language development during the elementary school period in terms of phonology, morphology, syntax, and semantics. The reader is aware that these facets of language do not exist in isolation; the division here is primarily for purposes of focus and more concentrated discussion.

Phonological Development. Most five year olds can correctly articulate most individual phonemes in most positions, but many have considerable difficulty combining a sequence of consonants in clusters (e.g., twel*fth*). Sounds in initial positions cause less difficulty than those in medial or final positions.

Plural forms such as *blocks* and *balloons* are typically produced at an earlier age than *es* forms such as *houses* or *busses,* and, as with most other phonological features, recognition precedes production. It appears that children perceive sounds in units—syllables and even words—and have difficulty producing component sounds. Palermo and Malfese report that "children have difficulty parsing the singular form from a plural form. . . . In the age range from 5 to 8 years, it would

---

24. Adrian Akmajian and Frank Heny, *An Introduction to Transformational Syntax* (Cambridge, Mass.: M.I.T. Press, 1975), p. 18.

appear that the word, or syllable, is the sound unit with which the child deals. He lacks the analytic abilities required to isolate and manipulate phonemic units within words."[25] The implications of these research findings for synthetic phonics approaches to reading and spelling instruction, to isolated sound-letter drill, are obvious. Palermo and Malfese conclude: "The child may have developed a complex system of phonological rules by the time he is six or seven years old, but he still has not abstracted the phoneme from that system of rules and mastered the complex relationships which it has to acoustic stimuli and to articulatory movements."[26]

Morphological Development. Studies of children's acquisition of pluralization rules have already been referred to; phonology and morphology are very closely related, obviously. Jean Berko's study will be briefly referred to because of the insights it provides regarding the development of morphological generalizations. She found that children gave consistent, although not always correct, answers to requests to supply plurals (This is a wug; here are two _____), verb tenses (This man is glinging; yesterday he _____), possessives (wug-wug's), and compounding (Why is a birthday called a birthday? "Because you get presents and eat cake"). Berko found few sex differences, but she did find some differences between the responses of preschoolers and first graders. However, she did not consider these differences qualitatively significant.[27]

John Carroll notes that "the period from 3 to 8 is marked by considerable difficulty in learning irregular forms,[28] but the fact that analogical formations occur at all attests to the ability of the child to respond to patterning in language at an early age."[29]

Syntactic Development. Paula Menyuk summarizes her extensive study of language development in children from four to seven as follows:

> The outstanding developments that occur in the sentences that children produce over the age range of approximately 4 to 7 years are (1) further expansion of base structure nodes (increase in class membership), (2) observation of selectional constraints or the co-occurrence of members of a class (observation of syntactic properties and combinatorial rules of lexical items), and (3) application of the syntactic operations of addition, deletion, substitution, and permutation to underlying sentences, as well as to items in a single underlying string. These developments probably continue well beyond age 5.[30]

---

25. David Palermo and Dennis Malfese, "Language Acquisition from Age Five Onward" (Paper presented to the Third Annual Michigan Conference on Applied Linguistics, January 30, 1971), p. 8.

26. Ibid.

27. Jean Berko, "The Child's Learning of English Morphology," in *Psycholinguistics: A Book of Readings,* ed. Sol Saporta (New York: Holt, Rinehart & Winston, 1961), pp. 359–71.

28. *bring-bringed*
   throw-throwed

29. John Carroll, "Language Development in Children," in *Psycholinguistics: A Book of Readings,* ed. Sol Saporta (New York: Holt, Rinehart & Winston, 1961), p. 335.

30. Paula Menyuk, *Sentences Children Use* (Cambridge, Mass.: M.I.T. Press, 1969), p. 151.

Five to seven year olds, she notes, have difficulty with pronominalization (To whom does *he* refer in a sentence such as "When Bob went to the store for mother, *he* forgot to buy milk"), *if* and *so* conjunctions (other researchers add to this list *although* and *because,* with *because* learned first, in a typical developmental pattern), and don't exhibit full development of the *have* auxiliary.[31]

Loban's work is probably well known by the reader and will only be summarized briefly here. In general, he noted the following trends in the language development of children involved in his longitudinal study. As subjects matured:

1. The occurrence of incomplete grammatical structures decreased.
2. A greater variety of sentence patterns was used.
3. There was greater variation in the structures within sentences.

Loban concludes: "From one school year to another, the amount of meaningful language or communication units increases slowly and gradually throughout the primary school year and then spurts forward at the fifth grade level."[32] Loban is one of several writers and researchers who comment on the coincidence of the child's arrival at new levels of language development at a point in time identified by Piaget as significant in cognitive development—in this case, the initial phases of the stage of formal operations.

Kellogg Hunt studied changes which occurred in the use of "T units" (minimal terminable units, similar to what Loban labeled communication units) as children progressed from the fourth grade through high school. Findings from Hunt's second study confirmed his convictions that T unit length is a better index of syntactic maturity than sentence length. Analyses of the writing of children and adolescents in the fourth, sixth, eighth, tenth, and twelfth grades showed that T unit length increased steadily, but number of T units per sentence decreased.[33] Hunt concludes:

> Successively older writers reduce more inputs to less than a predicate (and) use a wider variety of transformations in doing so. This greater variety indicates that older writers have a wider variety of syntactic resources to draw upon. One can scarcely escape the conclusion that as writers mature, they take advantage of more and more opportunities for consolidating sentences.[34]

Results of Carol Chomsky's study of the sequential acquisition of selected syntactic structures are probably well known and will only be reviewed here. Structures studied were as follows:

1. John is easy to see. (Who is the subject of the sentence? What is the subject of *see?*)
2. John promised Bill to go. (Who is the subject of *go?*)
3. John asked Bill what to do. (Who is the subject of *do?*)
4. He knew that John was going to win the race. (Who is the reference of *he?*)

31. Ibid., p. 115.

32. Walter Loban, *Stages, Velocity, and Prediction of Language Development—Kindergarten Through Grade Twelve* (Washington, D.C.: Office of Education, Bureau of Research, 1970), p. 33.

33. Kellogg Hunt, "Syntactic Maturity in School Children and Adults," *Monographs of the Society for Research in Child Development,* 1970, 35 (Serial No. 112).

34. Ibid., p. 53.

Chomsky reports that structures one, two, and three are strongly subject to individual rates of development. Structures one and two are acquired between 5.6 and 9 years and were known by all those children 9 and over who were tested. Structure three was not known by all children even at age 10, and the last structure was known by almost all children at age 5.6. She concludes: "Contrary to the commonly held view that a child has mastered the structures of his native language by the age of six, we find that active syntactic acquisition is taking place up to the age of nine and perhaps even beyond."[35]

Kessel studied the acquisition of similar structures, and his findings were not markedly different from Chomsky's. Palermo and Malfese note that "the major difference was that Kessel's subjects tended to achieve the various stages described by Chomsky at somewhat earlier stages. Like Chomsky, Kessel found that children passed through an invariant and nontransitive sequence in their acquisition of ask and tell."[36]

Semantic Development. Much of the research reviewed previously relates directly to the child's cognitive development, his relationships to his expanding environment, and his ability to categorize, to see relationships, and to order his linguistic equipment adequately in order to communicate his reactions to all that he experiences. Semantics cannot really be separated from the other areas just discussed—meanings directly influence sounds and their relationships (phonology), the ability to manipulate words or parts of words (morphology), and the way the words are arranged in utterances or sentences (syntax). Comprehension of meaning is of major significance, whether the message is oral or written. Carol Chomsky's work has obvious importance for teachers of reading—we too often overestimate children's ability to comprehend pronominalization or to make promise-tell distinctions in the material they read.

It seems that passive and negative sentences present some comprehension problems in both the production and reception facets of language. Passive sentences appear to be easier when the nouns are nonreversible. (Food was eaten by girls.)

As noted before, young elementary school pupils have only incomplete knowledge of such connectives as *and, or, therefore, although,* and *because.* Palermo and Malfese summarize the data for these terms as follows:

> While the first grader may use these words in his spontaneous speech, it would appear that the temporal relations of because, for example, are better understood than the causal ones. . . . In other words all of these words are used as if they were marked semantically as *then.* In addition, it appeared that when the adversative connectives *but* and *although* were used, children in the first grade showed little evidence of comprehending such constructions, and the sixth graders, while better in the identification of sentences correctly using the words, showed little ability to account for their choice. Finally, there was a developmental trend revealing an increase from Grade 1 to Grade 6 in the preference for the linguistic order of clauses to mirror the temporal order of cause and effect events.[37]

---

35. Carol Chomsky, *The Acquisition of Syntax in Children from Five to Ten* (Cambridge, Mass.: M.I.T. Press, 1969).

36. Palermo and Malfese, "Language Acquisition from Age Five Onward," p. 12.

37. Ibid., p. 16.

Rohwer and Bean studied children's and adolescents' abilities to recall noun pairs. Although children learned noun pairs presented in sentences more readily than noun pairs presented alone, this difference was not apparent in the performance of college students.[38]

Studies of vocabulary development, word associations, word recognition, and recall of word strings indicate that both horizontal and vertical growth continue throughout the elementary school period; that is, children continue to mature both in size of vocabularies (and in utilizing the number of ways for combining these words) and in adding depth to their understanding of the processes involved.

Several conclusions appear to be warranted on the basis of this very brief review of recent studies of children's linguistic development.

1. Language development, although well advanced by the age of school entrance, is far from complete.
2. Growth occurs in all the areas identified—phonology, morphology, syntax, and semantics.
3. There are probably some close corollaries between cognitive growth and linguistic development. The results of several studies suggest that growth spurts and plateaus parallel the well-known Piagetian stages; ages five (toward the beginning of the concrete operations period) and eleven (roughly approximating the beginning of the formal operations stage) seem to be very significant periods in language development. Further research in this area is clearly needed, perhaps best conducted by those not already convinced of the validity of the Piagetian viewpoint.
4. Teachers' expectations in terms of reading comprehension, skill in composition, and the acquisition of phoneme-grapheme correspondence generalizations should be adjusted to account for the growth still occurring. Specifically, it should not be surprising if some third graders have difficulty with comprehending the full implications of an *although* clause, or if six year olds are limited to *and* and *then* as means of combining sentences or clauses.

Some Implications of Linguistics for Elementary Teaching

Linguists have uncovered a mass of data regarding the operation and structure of language. They have devoted years to studying the changes that have occurred, to analyzing languages and developing superior methods and techniques for making such analyses. It is probably clear that no modern elementary teacher of the language arts would intentionally disregard such a significant body of knowledge. Yet, what difference does all this make? How will the elementary teacher change his methods of teaching speaking, reading, and spelling as a result of the linguistic advances reported in this chapter? The elementary teacher may feel that the information in the preceding section contributes to his background knowledge and

38. William Rohwer and Joan Bean, "Sentence Effects and Noun-Pair Learning: A Developmental Interaction During Adolescence," *Journal of Experimental Child Psychology* 15 (1973): 521–33.

that his general education has profited by reading about the history of our language and about the contributions of important linguistic scientists. One's coffee-room conversation may "sparkle" a bit more, and one's fellow teachers may be favorably impressed if the reader mentions the continual borrowing from Latin in coining new words to label our scientific and technological advances. But, really, isn't this about as far as it goes? If linguists disagree about the importance of a phoneme, if not everyone agrees with the ways in which transformational grammar differs from transformational-generative and case grammars, what can the elementary teacher (who has taken, perhaps, fifteen semester hours of course work in speech, composition, and literature and one course in teaching language arts) find to apply to his own teaching?

In a sense, this entire book represents a search for the answer to that question; a major purpose of this book is to seek out and record some findings from the field of linguistics and to point out their relevance and/or application to the teaching of reading, writing, spelling, speaking, and listening in the elementary school. In the chapters that follow, the implications of linguistic research for teaching these areas of the language arts will be discussed in some detail. In general, and as an introductory statement which can serve as an overview of this book, the implications might be summarized as follows:

1. Because we know that language is arbitrary and changing, a teacher's attitude toward nonstandard usage should be one of acceptance. Acceptance of a child from a culturally different background necessitates accepting the child's language. Otherwise communication between the child and teacher is seriously hampered; in some cases, it ceases to exist. However, techniques for changing the child's language may be employed in order that his opportunities to advance socially will not be thwarted, that he will *not* be kept from getting a scholarship to a college he very much wants to attend, or kept from being hired to do a job he is well equipped to do. Acceptance of a pupil's language is a necessary beginning, a prerequisite to all classroom work done in language. Language is such an intensely personal characteristic—only pause to think how one feels when a minor grammatical error is corrected by a peer or a "superior." Although we should know better, criticism of our language ("Gee you say that funny—say it again!") is generally accepted as criticism on a more general and personal level.

   One level of language is not "better" than another; this is why the term *nonstandard* is preferable to *substandard* in describing such usage as "He don't do it," "Was you there?" A person who uses terms such as these will probably be penalized in terms of social and educational advancement in our society, however, and it is for this reason that the teacher helps children work toward, and eventually achieve, standard usage, perhaps as a "second" language.

   Standards change and what is correrct today may be "prissy" or pedantic within a few years. For example, *whom* is in a state of rapid decline; linguists tell us it will probably leave our language before the time of our great-grand-children. Many scholars accept "It's me" as well as "It's I," and grammar books used by children in 2076 may, and probably will, list "It's me" as standard.

2. The study of language, with the knowledge that it is an exciting, growing, changing organism, will be more interesting to children when grammarians no longer act as though they were members of a mythical American equivalent of the French Academie, setting precise standards for our language and telling us that statement A is more "correct" than statement B. Even a quick perusal of language textbooks reveals advice that impedes, rather than aids, communication, and patterns that are quite unnatural.

3. With reference to oral language, the classroom teacher will devote much more time to causing children to engage in conversations, discussions, oral reading, dramatic plays, and choral speaking. Something in excess of 80 percent of most adults' language experiences are in the speaking-listening area, and teachers can be much more effective than they presently are in helping children learn to use these important skills more effectively. Vocabulary growth is important here, and so is intonation; children can learn a great deal about pitch, stress, and juncture as clues to meaning, and they can then apply what they know to making their own speech more colorful and interesting. The skills involved are acquired, not inborn, and teachers have a responsibility to aid and abet the continuous acquisition of oral language skills.

4. In the area of listening, children can analyze the way a speaker has *used* pitch, stress, juncture, and kinesis to convey meaning, exaggerate facts, or conceal points of weakness. Critical listening—"auding," if you will—depends upon the ability to spot or identify the speaker's use of the devices just mentioned to sway his audience (whether one or one hundred) to his way of thinking. John F. Kennedy is credited with noting that Winston Churchill "marshalled the English language and sent it to war." Adolph Hitler's use of invective, his repetition of half-truths and falsehoods so often they were accepted as facts, his ability to convince audiences that he alone could lead Germany to greatness, had a great deal to do with his success. In a democracy especially, the ability to use judgment in responding to a speaker is very important. Linguists have helped us do this by classifying the elements in oral discourse which speakers use in combining words to convey meaning. Teachers have frequently used the technique of comparing the way different newspapers reported the same news events; similar techniques have value in discussing speeches, newscasts, and so forth, which have been tape recorded or which children can hear or watch "live" on radio or television.

5. In reading, linguists have perhaps recommended more drastic changes than in any other area except grammar. Bloomfield, Fries, and H. L. Smith have wide differences of opinion on details, and some differences in basic principles, but in general they recommend:

  a. more emphasis, at an early level, on learning the alphabetic principle, if not the alphabet itself.

  b. a beginning vocabulary of words that follow consistent patterns—usually consonant-short vowel-consonant patterns (*pan, rug,* etc.).

  c. an absence of work on isolated speech sounds. It is almost impossible to repeat a consonant without following it with a vowel sound of some sort. Practice on isolated sounds usually proves to be of little value in oral reading that is natural. Sentences or groups of sentences make words, and sound elements of these words change with changing sentences. Linguists also tend to assign to oral reading a more prominent role, at least beyond the beginning stages. Reading is used as a tool for teaching intonation patterns and their role in determining meaning.

6. In spelling, linguists recommend the same emphasis on consistent patterns and would probably discard spelling lists consisting of words selected for their interest level or frequency of use by children. If some compromise can be developed, teachers could possibly do more toward helping children learn principles they could apply to unknown words as well as learning words they need to use at present. Teachers can expect changes in spelling programs, just as they can expect changes in reading programs. Most major publishers will not want the title page of a reading or spelling text printed without including the name of a linguist as an author or as a consultant to the author.

7. Children will learn to think of the dictionary as a device for recording what is in our language, rather than a set of standards or rules for what should be. It is with reference to the role and function of the dictionary that linguists have fought some of their most serious battles with those who hold a more traditional view of language. If the reader isn't familiar with the furor caused by publication of Webster's Third International Dictionary, he should be![39] Dictionary work will be more interesting for children if several dictionaries are used, and their systems of diacritical marking compared. This is not likely to happen if one dictionary is accepted as the sole arbiter in our language.

8. Finally, it is hoped that teachers will find that language study is fascinating, not dull or boring. The more a person knows about his language, the more he wants to know. Not only should the elementary teacher feel this enthusiasm and respond to it, but he should share this enthusiasm with children. If it is a genuine interest, he cannot help sharing it. Children will enjoy inventing new words, studying the derivations of words, learning something of the history of their language, and analyzing their own sentence patterns. The problem, in a self-contained classroom, may become one of balance—other curricular areas are important, too!

Summary

In establishing the objectives or purposes of this book, it was noted that the elementary teacher is told that *this* reading program, or *that* spelling series is "linguistically sound." Thus, establishing some criteria for evaluating this "soundness" seems to be important. Far-reaching changes are suggested in teaching grammar and in differentiating grammar and usage. The elementary teacher expresses some concern and wonders if it is true that standards of usage are being absolutely *abolished*. Linguists can provide some data which may relieve this anxiety somewhat.

Linguists are slowly making their influence felt in the language arts curricula of

---

39. Albert Marckwardt, "Dictionaries and the English Language," *The English Journal* 52 (1963): 336–45.

elementary schools. The problem facing the elementary teacher is one of selectivity, of determining which of the many linguistic proposals are most attuned to what is known about elementary school children and how they learn; which principles are the most durable, the most significant, those with which students of the English language should be aware. This book is written in order to help the elementary teacher gain some knowledge of his language and of linguists' efforts to study language scientifically. Another purpose is to assist the classroom teacher in applying appropriate portions of linguistic knowledge to his teaching—his methods, techniques, and the materials he selects.

A brief history of the development of the English language was included. Points of emphasis included the contributions of the Anglo-Saxons, the Danes, the Norman French; the contribution of the Latin language was discussed. Change and flexibility were identified as significant, not undesirable, characteristics of our language.

The work of a number of linguistic scientists was described very briefly. Some linguists have devoted most of their efforts to studying the sounds of language, others to studying the structure of language. Semanticists are interested in word meanings. Other linguists make their contribution by analyzing sounds, writing grammars, and developing writing systems for the speakers of the 3,000 to 5,000 languages of the world, the majority of which have not been written. A brief overview of the current evidence related to children's language development was included, as was the clear suggestion that elementary teachers should view children's language development as far from complete at the time of school entrance.

Finally, the possible implications of the work of linguists for the work of elementary classroom teachers was discussed. The problem of standards received some attention. Knowing that our language is arbitrary and changing should have some effect on the elementary teacher who has previously expected a level of language in the classroom which is unnatural and unlifelike.

Reading programs, at the beginning levels particularly, and spelling programs will feel the impact of linguists' work in phonology and syntax. Language in pre-primers is likely to be more natural and childlike in the future, and reading will not as frequently be taught as though it were only a visual process.

The role of the dictionary, and lessons on how to use it, will probably change somewhat. Its stature is not diminished when one admits that it is a recording of a language as it is, or was, at a given point in time.

Selected References

Akmajian, Adrian, and Frank Heny. *An Introduction to Transformational Syntax.* Cambridge, Mass.: M.I.T. Press, 1975.

Brown, Roger, and Ursula Bellugi. "Three Processes in the Child's Acquisition of Syntax." *Harvard Educational Review* 34(1969):133–51.

Burns, Paul, and Betty Broman. *The Language Arts in Childhood Education.* Chicago: Rand-McNally & Co., 1975.

Carroll, John. *Language and Thought.* Englewood Cliffs, N. J.: Prentice-Hall, 1964.

Chomsky, Carol. *The Acquisition of Syntax in Children from Five to Ten.* Cambridge, Mass.: M.I.T. Press, 1969.

Dineen, Francis. *An Introduction to General Linguistics.* New York: Holt, Rinehart & Winston, 1967.

Emig, Janet. "Children and Metaphor." *Research in the Teaching of English* 2(1972): 163–71.

Fodor, Jerry, and Jerrold Katz. *The Structure of Language.* Englewood Cliffs, N. J.: Prentice-Hall, 1964.

Francis, W. Nelson. "Revolution in Grammar." In *Readings in Applied English Linguistics,* pp. 69–84. Englewood Cliffs, N. J.: Prentice-Hall, 1964.

_____. *The Structure of American English.* New York: Ronald Press Co., 1958.

Fries, Charles. *Linguistics and Reading.* New York: Holt, Rinehart & Winston, 1963.

Girsdansky, Michael. *The Adventure of Language.* Englewood Cliffs, N. J.: Prentice-Hall, 1963.

Gleason, Henry. *Linguistics and English Grammar.* New York: Holt, Rinehart & Winston, 1965.

Hall, Robert. *Linguistics and Your Language.* Garden City, N.Y.: Doubleday & Co., Anchor Books, 1960.

Hanf, Marilyn. "A Study of Children's Language as Expressed Through Oral Language Discourse." *Research in the Teaching of English* 7(1973):13–39.

Hunt, Kellogg. "Syntactic Maturity in Children and Adults." *Monographs of the Society for Research in Child Development,* 1970, *35* (Serial No. 112).

Ianni, Lawrence. "An Answer to Doubts about the Usefulness of the New Grammar." *The English Journal* 53(1964):597–602.

Jesperson, Otto. *Growth and Structure of the English Language.* New York: Macmillan Co., 1938.

Joos, Martin. "Language and the School Child." *Harvard Educational Review* 34(1964): 203–10.

Koziol, Stephen. "The Development of Noun Plural Rules During the Primary Grades." *Research in the Teaching of English* 7(1973):30–50.

Loban, Walter. *Stages, Velocity, and Prediction of Language Development—Kindergarten Through Grade 12.* Washington, D.C.: U.S. Office of Education, Bureau of Research, 1970.

Menyuk, Paula. *Sentences Children Use.* Cambridge, Mass.: M.I.T. Press, 1969.

Palermo, David, and Dennis Malfese. "Language Acquisition from Age Five Onward." Paper presented to the Third Annual Michigan Conference on Applied Linguistics, 30 January 1971. Mimeographed.

Pope, Mike. "Syntactic Maturity of Black and White Fourth Graders' Speech." *Research in the Teaching of English* 7(1973):30–50.

_____. "The Syntax of Fourth Graders' Narrative and Explanatory Speech." *Research in the Teaching of English* 8(1974):219–27.

Roberts, Paul. *English Sentences.* New York: Harcourt Brace Jovanovich, 1962.

Rohwer, William, and Joan Bean. "Sentence Effects and Noun-Pair Learning: A Developmental Interaction During Adolescence." *Journal of Experimental Child Psychology* 15(1973):521–33.

Saporta, Sol, ed. *Psycholinguistics: A Book of Readings.* New York: Holt, Rinehart & Winston, 1961.

Shafer, Robert. "What Teachers Should Know About Children's Language." *Elementary English* 52(1975):498–501.

Smith, Frank, and George Miller, eds. *The Genesis of Language.* Cambridge, Mass.: M.I.T. Press, 1966.

Strang, Barbara. *Modern English Structure.* London: Edward Arnold Publishers, 1962.

West, Fred. *The Way of Language.* New York: Harcourt Brace Jovanovich, 1975.

Materials for Children

Brown, Ivor. *Shakespeare and His World.* New York: Henry Walck, 1967.

Elles, John. *They Lived Like This in Chaucer's England.* New York: Franklin Watts, 1967.

Folsom, Franklin. *The Language Book.* New York: Grosset & Dunlap, 1963.

Grohskopf, Bernice. *From Age to Age: Life and Literature in Chaucer's England.* New York: Atheneum Publishers, 1968.

Hamilton, Franklin. *1066.* New York: Dial Press, 1964.

Harris, Brayton. *Johann Gutenberg and the Invention of Printing.* New York: Franklin Watts, 1974.

O'Neil, Mary. *Words, Words, Words.* Garden City, N.Y.: Doubleday & Co., 1966.

Provenson, Alice, and Martin Provenson. *Karen's Opposites.* New York: Golden Press, 1963.

Sparke, William. *The Story of the English Language.* New York: Abelard-Schuman, 1965.

2

Linguistics and Reading

Linguists continue to be among the most severe and productive critics of current methods and materials for reading instruction. They claim superiority for programs they have developed, or, at least, points of view they espouse, because their programs are based upon carefully gathered and analyzed data regarding our language. David Reed very clearly states the position held by many linguists:

> In order to discuss reading from a linguistic point of view, it is important to distinguish between the elementary aspects of reading (termed here "the process of reading") and what reading specialists are accustomed to think of as more advanced aspects of the same subject (which may be termed "the uses of reading"). Children with normal physical and mental capacity, whose sociocultural backgrounds are not severely disadvantaged, ought to master the process of reading by the end of their second year in school. That is to say, such children ought to be able by that time to identify, through viewing the graphic symbols by which linguistic forms are conventionally represented in writing, all the linguistic forms by hearing the phonological symbols by which the same forms are represented in speech. In contrast, no one freely masters the uses of reading in a lifetime devoted to that discipline."[1]

Linguists have rather consistently viewed the separation of *process* from *use* as essential in making reading instruction, especially in the initial stages, more effective

---

1. David Reed, "Linguistic Forms and the Process of Reading," in *Basic Studies in Reading,* ed. Harry Levin and Joanna Williams (New York: Basic Books, 1970), p. 19.

and efficient. The majority of linguists also concur with David Reed's emphasis upon the child's major or fundamental task: associating already comprehended sound patterns with related visual patterns. There is much less agreement on the precise dimensions of the "chunks," visual and auditory, which are to be processed. Is it grapheme and phoneme or utterance and sentence? Noam Chomsky writes: "It may very well be that one of the best ways to teach reading is to enrich the child's vocabulary so that he constructs for himself the deeper representations of sound that correspond so closely to orthographic forms."[2] Clearly, Chomsky is concerned with units larger than the phoneme and the grapheme.

Among the most significant contributions to the literature on reading instruction have been those made by Leonard Bloomfield, Charles Fries, and Henry L. Smith. These linguists, usually classified as "structuralists," have related the findings of scholars in their field to the reading process and have developed instructional programs. The essential elements of these programs will be summarized and discussed in this chapter.

The more recent contributions of psycholinguists and sociolinguists will be reviewed, and reference will be made to the variety of points of view regarding the size of the decoding unit basic to reading.

It is important to note that linguists are primarily concerned with the scientific study of language, its history, and/or its present structure. They view the reading process from a somewhat different perspective than do those reading authorities whose advice has been sought, and heeded, in the past. Linguists are not professional educators, and few of them have struggled with the problems regularly encountered by classroom teachers as they attempt to teach large groups of children to read. Nevertheless, linguists' proposals deserve to be studied, objectively and carefully. The results of such study may be the adoption of a "linguistic" program, or the adaptation and incorporation of principles, concepts, or techniques from several such programs. All the evidence regarding the effectiveness of linguistic reading programs should be evaluated in the light of our knowledge of the reading process and all those who engage in the process.

All linguistic reading programs are not the same. Specifically, the programs developed by Bloomfield, Fries, and H. L. Smith are based on differing positions regarding the use of the alphabet in beginning reading, the role of isolated word drill, and the importance of oral reading. Therefore, it is of some significance to indicate whose linguistic program is being discussed or evaluated.

Despite rather clear differences in point of view, in program and methodological recommendations, and in degree of emphasis on meaning, or comprehension, at beginning levels, linguists are serious students of language, and their concepts, criticisms, and recommendations related to reading deserve to be taken seriously by educators.

The Reading Process Defined

Most linguists propose a somewhat different definition of reading than has been accepted by reading specialists in the past. Clarence L. Barnhart, writing in *Let's*

---

2. Noam Chomsky, "Phonology and Reading," in *Basic Studies in Reading*, p. 18.

Read, one of the first major efforts to relate linguistic science to problems of reading instruction, defines reading as follows:

> Bloomfield's system of teaching reading is a linguistic system. *Essentially, a linguistic system of teaching reading separates the problem of the study of word-form from the study of word-meaning.* Most children, when they enter school, know at least 5000 words, many of them know 10,000 words, and in the opinion of some investigators, some know as many as 20,000 or 25,000 words. The child's knowledge of words and their meanings is much more wide-spread when he enters school than most teachers and parents realize. The child has had five or six years' experience in acquiring meanings, and he uses them readily in many kinds of syntactical patterns. He knows how to speak the English language, but he does not know how to read the forms of words. These forms are usually presented in a hit-or-miss fashion dependent upon the content of the various stories that are presented to him. Bloomfield felt that new words should be presented according to their form; that is, regular forms should be presented first, irregular forms only later. By getting all the associated facts together, the child's power to recognize words in his reading is greatly facilitated. After learning the first list or two, a child should be able to learn a whole list of words almost as rapidly as he learns one word now by means of the word method. In Bloomfield's system that child is engaged in relating the sound of a word to the form of the word in print.[3]

Later in this chapter, the Bloomfield system will be described in more detail and some of its implications suggested. The point to be underscored here is the stress Bloomfield places on reading as a process of correlating a sound image with its corresponding visual image or its spelling. Reading, according to Bloomfield, has little to do with getting meaning from a printed page. Sending and receiving messages, encoding and decoding, are language processes, not confined merely to the language process called reading. The unit to be decoded, in the beginning stages at least, is a word or wordlike pattern in which the relationship between sound and letter can be clearly seen (and heard).

Charles Fries takes essentially the same position. Learning to read is *not* a process of learning new language signals, or signals other than those the child has already learned. The signals are the same; the difference lies in the medium through which the physical stimuli make contact with the child's nervous system. In "talk," the physical stimuli of the language signals make their contact by means of sound waves received by the ear. In reading, the physical stimuli of the same language signals consist of graphic shapes that make their contact with the nervous system through light waves received by the eye.

> The process of learning to read in one's native language is *the process of transfer* from the auditory signs for language signals, which the child has already learned, to the new visual signs for the same signals.[4]

Carl LeFevre takes issue with Fries and with Bloomfield, and his basic premises regarding reading materials differ from theirs. However, like Fries and Bloomfield,

---

3. Leonard Bloomfield and Clarence Barnhart, *Let's Read: A Linguistic Approach* (Detroit: Wayne State University Press, 1961), pp. 9–10. Italics not in original text.

4. Charles Fries, *Linguistics and Reading* (New York: Holt, Rinehart & Winston, 1963), p. 120.

LeFevre places a great deal of emphasis on helping the child establish automatic relationships between sounds and printed symbols. LeFevre writes:

> While aware of complex causations, I believe misapprehending the relationships between spoken and printed language patterns, a problem that can be illuminated by linguistic insights—to be the most decisive element in reading failures.[5]

The reader is undoubtedly aware of definitions which suggest that reading is primarily a process of getting meaning from the printed page. Methods variously, and sometimes inaccurately, called the "look-say" method, the "sight" method, the "word" method (and not infrequently today, the "reading by guesswork" method) place strong emphasis upon the use of context clues, pictures, and configuration in deciphering or decoding a writer's message. Russell Stauffer contends:

> Reading is a mental process requiring accurate word recognition, ability to call to mind particular meanings, and ability to shift or reassociate meanings—until the constructs or concepts presented are clearly grasped, or rejected. This means that knowledge gained through reading can increase understanding and, in turn, influence social and personal adjustment, enrich experience, and stimulate thinking.[6]

Linguists, typically, would contend that Dr. Stauffer, and others with similarly broad and general definitions of reading, are making the mistake of confusing the *uses* of reading with the reading process itself. Stauffer, of course, could not agree.

Reading Methods of the Past

The reader is probably aware that children were taught to read in colonial times primarily to ensure the salvation of their souls through exposure to the Bible and other revelations from God. The materials used were religious stories and, as skills improved, the Bible itself. This was the era of the *New England Primer*—"In Adam's fall we sinn-ed all"—and spelling aloud each letter of a word was a commonly used technique for "word analysis."

Noah Webster's contribution to reading instruction, the *Blue-Back Speller*, followed the *New England Primer* as a basic text and was used until about 1840. Stories with a patriotic emphasis replaced the religious material of the colonial era.

The so-called word method became popular in this country in the last half of the nineteenth century, after visits by American educators (Horace Mann among them) to schools in Prussia and Switzerland where this method was being used successfully. These educators returned to the United States strongly advocating the use of the word method instead of the highly phonic approach employed by Webster. The word method, which relied upon building word-picture or word-object

---

5. Carl LeFevre, *Linguistics and the Teaching of Reading* (New York: McGraw-Hill, 1964), pp. 4–6.

6. Russell Stauffer, *Directing Reading Maturity as a Cognitive Process* (New York: Harper & Row, 1969), p. 16.

associations, lasted for at least forty-five years (some claim it is alive and well today!), to be supplanted by methods utilizing phonics to a greater extent. It would be a serious error to assume that sounds and their study were ever eliminated from reading instruction. Phonics has had its up and downs, but it has never really disappeared.

The years from 1925 to 1935 and the period following World War II have several characteristics in common. Reading instruction assumed a role of greater depth and breadth, with a wider utilization of a variety of methods. Teachers became more interested in using materials which had literary merit and which were similar to those materials which were used by adults—namely, newspapers and magazines.

Returning to the "phonics" versus "look-say" issue, it might be said that at the present time the approach most commonly used might be termed an "eclectic" approach, using not one method, but a combination of methods. Contemporary adults who claim never to have been taught phonics outnumber by several hundred to one the number of elementary teachers who claim not to teach phonics. The cry of Flesch, and others, that phonics has been ignored is rather difficult to support if one takes the time and makes the effort to visit elementary classrooms. Teachers today teach not only the phonics skills requisite for success in reading the most popular basal readers, but many use a separate phonics workbook and include in their daily programs a "phonics" period in addition to periods devoted to reading and spelling instruction in which phonics may also receive some emphasis. Very few elementary teachers today ignore giving instruction in the sound–written-symbol relationships which linguists advocate. Certainly, there appears to be little or no support for the accusation that too little time is devoted to instruction in phonics in the majority of elementary classrooms. Whether the phonics work on which teachers and children spend so much time and energy is *linguistically sound* is another issue, and one which should be dealt with promptly.

Bloomfield and Barnhart criticize most highly phonic approaches to reading instruction on two bases. First, they indicate that *producing* a particular speech sound in isolation is confusing for some youngsters and unnecessary. Work on sound–written-symbol relationships is premature if the child cannot hear and utter the significant sounds as they occur in words. Most six-year-old children "have no need whatever of the drill which is given by phonic methods."[7]

Their second criticism is based on the isloation of speech sounds, which occurs in most phonics programs. There is little value in pronouncing the letter *p* in isolation; it is almost impossible to do this—a vowel of some sort almost inevitably follows the pronunciation of any consonant. The initial consonant sound in the word *pie* is not the same as the initial consonant sound in the word *poor,* and when this consonant sound is moved to medial or final positions, the variation is even greater. Most linguists agree the ability to pronounce successfully a long series of isolated initial consonants and consonant blends has little relationship to successful reading.[8]

Ronald Wardhaugh, a contemporary and highly regarded linguist (and the

---

7. Bloomfield and Barnhart, *Let's Read,* p. 27.
8. Fries, *Linguistics and Reading,* p. 146.

author/consultant for a major basal reading series) lists the following criticisms of most phonics programs:

What is the writer condemning? He is condemning the following kinds of statements because each is *linguistically* indefensible:

1. Statements about letters having sounds; as, for example, "these letters must be blended to arrive at the correct sound." Letters are letters and sounds are sounds; they must not be confused with each other.

2. Statements about syllabication which apply only to word-breaking conventions in printing when these statements are made into rules of pronunciation, as when butter is broken into *but* and *ter* and monkey into *mon* and *key*. There is only one medial consonant in *butter* and its phonetic quality derives from its relationship to both vowels in the word, not just the first.

3. Statements about slurring, poor enunciation, incorrect articulation, and mis-pronunciation, as when *doing* is said to be "incorrectly" pronounced if said as *doin'*. A whole set of such shibboleths exists.

4. Statements about "long" and "short" vowels, as when *mad* is said to have a short vowel and *made* (sic) a long vowel (even though in any pronunciation the writer has heard the second vowel is shorter in duration than the first!) Allophonic vowel length depends upon whether the vowel is final or non-final in a word or whether it is followed by a voiced or voiceless consonant. There might be something like "long" and "short" vowels in English but they are nothing like those in the books on reading.

5. Statements about teaching children the sounds of their language, as though they did not already know these (for how else could they speak?).

6. Statements which do not allow for well-known dialect variations, as when the word *when* is always taught as /hwen/ no matter which part of the United States the child comes from, or *due* as /dyuw/ or *pin* and *pen* which cannot be /pin/.

The preceding is just a list of some of the readily observable weaknesses of the phonics instruction that has proved, according to Diack, Mathews and Chall, to be superior to other kinds of instruction. It is a mixture of fact and fiction. Description and prescription go hand-in-hand, but the teacher apparently never knows which is which. Speech and writing are confused. The teaching of reading is associated with the teaching of some kind of proper language, but the latter is never precisely defined. Worse still, there is more teaching about what the writer will call an artificial and haphazard set of observations, or generalizations, than teaching of the desired responses.[9]

Wardhaugh concludes:

Anyone seriously interested in teaching children to read must be prepared to acquire a knowledge of the phonological system of English. He must also find out how that system is represented in English orthography; how people, particularly six-year olds, actually speak; and how such speech varies in the different dimensions of social and regional dialects. He must also be aware that children know their language when they come to school (for they can speak) and that grammatical and lexical knowl-

9. Ronald Wardhaugh, "The Teaching of Phonics and Comprehension: A Linguistic Evaluation," in *Psycholinguistics and the Teaching of Reading,* ed. Kenneth Goodman and James Fleming (Newark, Del.: International Reading Association, 1969), p. 82. Reprinted with permission of Ronald Wardhaugh and the International Reading Association.

edge as well as phonological knowledge is brought by children to the task of reading.[10]

A bit of interesting irony will serve to close this brief review of reading instruction practices in elementary schools in the United States. The reader is asked to note carefully the lesson copied from McGuffey's *First Eclectic Reader* (copyright 1920) and to compare it with this lesson from *Let's Read* (copyright 1961).

> Lesson II—McGuffey's *First Eclectic Reader*
> Is the cat on the mat?
> The cat is on the mat.[11]

> Lesson 2—*Let's Read*
> Can Pat fan Dan?
> Pat can fan Dan.
> Nan can pat a cat.
> A fat rat ran.[12]

Observing these two selections, the elementary teacher might have a difficult time answering the question, "What's new in reading instruction?"

The Alphabet and Beginning Reading

In most linguistic methods of teaching reading, much emphasis is placed on beginning with the alphabet. Bloomfield and Barnhart write:

> The first step, which may be divorced from all subsequent ones, is the recognition of the letters. We say that a child *recognizes* a letter when he can, upon request, make some response to it . . . The conventional responses to the sight of the letters are their names, *aye, bee, see,*[13] *dee, ee, eff,* and so on. . . . There is not the slightest reason for using any other responses.

They continue:

> The child should be familiar with all the letters, capital and small, of the printed alphabet before reading is begun. Not all of them will be used in the first reading work, but we do not want the reading work, at any stage, to be upset by the appearance of unfamiliar shapes.[14]

---

10. Ibid., p. 85.
11. William McGuffey, *First Eclectic Reader*, rev. ed. (New York: American Book Co., 1920), p. 8.
12. Bloomfield and Barnhart, *Let's Read*, p. 61. In fairness, it should be pointed out that the *Let's Read* lesson is not included in its entirety. Even so, the reader is left to decide for herself the degree of progress indicated by these two examples.
13. What happens when the child is exposed to *c* as in *coat, catch,* and *come* or *g* as in *gift* and *gambling*? "Calling" letters of the alphabet may create a number of problems as well as possibly solving some.
14. Bloomfield and Barnhart, *Let's Read*, p. 35.

Fries is also adamant regarding the importance of learning the letters of the alphabet, although he restricts the shapes children should learn to capital letters. Unlike Bloomfield, Fries does not advocate learning the names of the letters:

> To learn the "letters" often means pronouncing the names in order to "spell" words. This again contributes little in the beginning stage of reading.
>
> But learning the letters may mean learning to identify and distinguish the graphic shapes that represent the written word-patterns. This ability to identify and distinguish the graphic shapes does not necessarily mean attaching the conventional names to these distinctive shapes, although the names are very useful as one means of checking the identification response. It is, however, *essential to reading at the very beginning* that pupils have already developed such an ability to *identify and distinguish the graphic shapes of the letters as can be shown by instant and automatic responses of recognition.*[15]

In other words, Fries considers it essential that children recognize significant differences in the shapes of letters; if they also learn to attach letter names to these shapes, this is a bonus.

LeFevre places somewhat less emphasis on learning the alphabet. He suggests that this will be a natural outgrowth of interest in language on the part of the child.

> In connection with reading readiness, it is interesting that some pre-school children undoubtedly learn to read by their own spelling method. Not so lucky as children who have listened to enchanting books read aloud to them by fond adults, such children nevertheless learn for themselves that words are graphic representations of things they can see and hear. They study the labels on boxes of soap or breakfast cereal, signs along the street, billboards, newspaper and magazine titles, television captions and advertising, anything and everything in print. They ask to hear what words these graphic symbols say. They ask how to spell the words. What are the letters, from left to right? How do you say the names of the letters? They say the words and the names of the letters aloud. They copy them. It is not much of a step for these children to ask how to reverse the process and write what they say. At this point they *do not need to be able to "sing" the alphabet as an arbitrary sequence of letters: they do know the alphabetic principle through knowing the names of many letters and some of the sounds the letters may represent.*[16]

It may seem to the reader that an undue amount of time has been spent discussing these linguists' positions relative to the alphabet. Before discussing specific recommendations regarding the content of beginning reading programs which are linguistically based, it seems important to clarify the role of knowledge of the alphabet in linguistic programs. As every experienced teacher knows, controversy has existed for some time regarding the importance of knowing the alphabet. (Indeed, specifying what was meant by "knowing" has been a problem in itself. Is it the ability to recall precise sequences of letters or the ability to "say" the names of the letters?)

---

15. Fries, *Linguistics and Reading*, p. 124.
16. LeFevre, *Linguistics and the Teaching of Reading*, p. 38. Italics not in original text.

i/t/a

No discussion of the problem of phoneme-grapheme correspondence would be complete without some attention to i/t/a, the initial teaching alphabet. Sir James Pitman is credited with the revision of his grandfather's phonemic alphabet to its present form. It is Pitman's premise that the sound–printed-symbol relationship is best taught and learned through the use of an "augmented" alphabet of forty-four symbols. A copy of this alphabet appears on page 34.

The intent of this alphabet is to reduce the confusion which occurs when one letter, *a,* for example, is used to represent a variety of sounds, as in *ate, apple, are,* and so forth. In materials printed in i/t/a, each *a* would be clearly distinguishable in its visual as well as its auditory form. In other words, the approach used is almost the opposite of those proposed by Bloomfield and Fries: control the alphabet (character system, to be more precise), and do what you like with the words! The child is freed, according to the supporters of i/t/a, to read and write more interesting stories and to use more interesting sentence patterns.

Proponents of i/t/a do not claim to present a "method" of teaching. On the contrary, they claim to present a *medium* through which reading can be taught by any method a teacher chooses. The additional symbols make teaching reading by a "phonetic" method more logical, and the symbols have been carefully designed to reduce the confusion which results when more visually oriented methods are used. There are no capital letters in i/t/a, and names and "sentence beginners" are indicated by i/t/a letters which have been darkened and enlarged.

It is difficult to evaluate i/t/a, because so much of the research regarding its effectiveness has been conducted by its supporters. Nevertheless, i/t/a represents a unique and interesting solution to the phoneme-grapheme problem which beginning readers encounter. Linguists appear to regard it positively, although with varying degrees of enthusiasm.

Intonation, Oral Reading, and Linguistic Approaches to Reading Instruction

In discussing the "swings of the pendulum" which have characterized reading instruction in the United States, reference was made to the emphasis, in colonial times, on having children spell aloud the words they were reading. The following advice is given to teachers using the phonics method with McGuffey's reader:

> First, teach the elementary sounds, and their representatives, the letters marked with diacriticals, as they occur in the lessons; then, the formation of words by the combination of these sounds . . . begin to teach the names of the letters and the spelling of words, and require the groups "a man," "a pen," "the pen," to be pronounced as a good reader would pronounce single words.[17]

---

17. McGuffey, *First Eclectic Reader,* rev. ed., p. ii. Such advice would—and does—horrify contemporary linguists. Almost without exception, they decry any pronunciation of words in isolation as part of a reading program. *A* pronounced in isolation has the sound of long *a* which is seldom a natural way of saying the word conversationally. The *e* in *the* is seldom a long *e* when used in context, "The book is on the table."

FIGURE 1

INITIAL TEACHING ALPHABET

(i/t/a)

Reprinted by permission of Initial Teaching Publications, Inc., New York.

Oral reading has had as many periods of emphasis and deemphasis as have other aspects of the reading program. During the period from about 1918 to 1925 when "sight" reading was most in vogue, oral reading was in much disrepute. It was assumed that oral reading interfered with comprehension and compounded the "word-calling" ills attributed to phonics. Teachers discovered, however, that oral reading served several useful purposes, the most important of which was to check the child's application of the several word-analysis skills she had been taught. Watching a child's eyes focus on a printed page and then to hear her intelligently discuss the content (such discussion was based, commonly, upon a highly developed ability to interpret pictures!) proved to be not altogether satisfactory in diagnosing reading problems or even being certain that the child was, in fact, reading. Oral reading has staged a comeback in the primary grades particularly, and linguists are not alone in advocating more emphasis upon oral reading.

Unfortunately, the reading materials linguists have prepared do not always reinforce what they write about the importance of intonation and of reading as one would talk. The following is part of Lesson Nine, from *Let's Read:*

> Dan had a big map.
> A big van sat at a dam.
> Sal had a big pig.[18]

The reader should decide whether or not such material gives full opportunity for reading with expression and using the full range of intonation skills. It should be noted that the picture brightens considerably in the more difficult materials prepared for pupils beyond the beginning levels.

Regardless of the materials used, it is the classroom teacher who must accept major responsibility for stressing the importance of intonation in meaningful oral reading. The teacher does not need a vast amount of linguistic knowledge in order to do this. Goodman writes: "Every time a teacher says to a child, 'Read that the way you would say it to a friend on the playground,' she is demonstrating that she senses the significance of natural intonation and its effect on comprehension."[19]

Of the authors whose materials and points of view have been referred to frequently throughout this chapter, LeFevre places the most stress on teaching reading in such a way that normal intonation and conversational stress and pitch will be supported, not violated. He writes:

> Underlying our language structure is intonation, yet our awareness of its importance is very recent. Most linguists agree that intonation is the structural feature that particularly distinguishes native accent from foreign. So far, the application of intonation data to the teaching of American English has been pretty well limited to punctuation, but it may turn out to be decisive in teaching American children to read their own language—as well as to write it more easily and efficiently.[20]

Several examples may serve to illustrate LeFevre's point. The reader should read *aloud* the following sentences to see clearly the differences—differences in stress, pitch, and pause, or juncture:

Please *record* the minutes of this meeting. (\ri-kòrd'\, used as a verb)

Play your new phonograph *record* again, won't you? (\rek'-ərd\, used as a noun)

Are you going to *school* today? (suggesting that it is an odd or unusual place to go today) (2-2-2-3-4)

Are *you* going to school today? (suggesting that it is unusual for you to go to school on this particular day) (2-3-2-2-4)

Are you going to school *today?* (suggesting that this *might* be an appropriate place to go tomorrow, or might have been an appropriate place to go yesterday, but there is some cause for surprise about going today) (2-2-2-2-4)

---

18. Bloomfield and Barnhart, *Let's Read*, p. 69.
19. Kenneth Goodman, "The Linguistics of Reading," *The Elementary School Journal* 63 (1964): 356.
20. LeFevre, *Linguistics and the Teaching of Reading*, p. 44.

The reader can supply many more examples of sentences in which the meaning is changed by a change in the word stressed or in the position of a juncture. A particularly ridiculous situation is suggested by one of the following sentences:

What's that in the road ahead?[21]

a head?

What's that in the road

(The joke can be made more obvious by a slight pause within *a-head* as well as stronger stress on *that* and *head*.)

These examples should make it abundantly clear that isolated word drill, or drill on words in structureless groupings arranged horizontally or vertically, in charts or on the chalkboard, can do little or nothing to improve children's ability to read aloud with intonation patterns which convey *their* meanings, let alone the author's.

Oral reading, using pitch, stress, and pause to convey meaning, is important and deserves a prominent role in reading programs in modern elementary schools, especially as part of the total assessment or evaluation program. Nevertheless, a major question is still unanswered. Most linguists also consider it important that children develop a basic understanding of the alphabet. Examples have been given suggesting that linguists *write* about the importance of intonation but have developed reading materials which make principles of intonation difficult to apply. What *do* the linguists recommend regarding oral reading? Bloomfield and Barnhart, it will be recalled, advocated naming each letter of the alphabet as a step in beginning reading. The process of reading the word *man* would go something like this:

1. "Bobby, what are the letters of this word?"
   Bobby responds (hopefully), "em-aye-en."
2. "Good! This word says *man*. Read it, please."
3. *"man."* Bobby responds correctly, and other words in the same pattern follow—*fan, dan, can.*

Bloomfield and Barnhart caution that writing or printing do not belong at this stage but will only confuse the child.[22]

It seems clear that in establishing the alphabetic principle (representing one sound with only one letter, at least at first) and in stressing the ability to name the letters of the alphabet as a prereading step, Bloomfield and Barnhart do little to aid children's reading aloud with appropriate stress and pitch and may, in fact, be doing violence to the natural language children bring to school with them. Bloomfield and Barnhart's best defense is one of their own paragraphs:

Reading is so familiar to us that we are likely to forget how difficult it is for the beginner. The child has so hard a time forming a connection between visual marks and speech sounds that he cannot attend to the meaning of what he reads. We must

---

21. This underlining represents another way of indicating pitch.
22. Bloomfield and Barnhart, *Let's Read*, p. 41.

help him to establish this connection, and we must not bother him, for the present, with anything else. We can best help him by giving him the most suitable words to read, and these are short words in which the letters have uniform values. We present as many as possible of these, *without regard to their meanings*. The child will get the meanings only when he has solved the mechanical problem of reading.[23]

Other linguists would suggest that Bloomfield and Barnhart's somewhat artificial approach *interferes* with reading since it is so unrelated to children's natural speech and does little to help them see the connection between speech and writing.

It is for this reason that Fries calls the initial stage of learning to read the "transfer" stage. By the transfer period, he means "the period during which the child is learning to transfer from the auditory signs for language signals, which he has already learned, to a set of visual signs for the same signals."[24]

Fries's steps with reference to beginning reading may be summarized as follows:

1. The development of the ability to contrast visual shapes presented as single capital letters, then combinations of capital letters in groups of two or three. The combinations of letters *need not* form words (AHE, TEM), and no attempt should be made to pronounce combinations of letters, even if they should happen to form words (FIT, HAT).
2. When the child has completely mastered the contrastive visual patterns, the teacher presents and pronounces contrastive word patterns //AT-CAT// //CAT-RAT//.

Although Bloomfield and Barnhart defend the presentation and pronunciation of nonsense syllables, Fries insists that the patterns used, at least beyond the introductory stage, should represent real words, words the child already knows, and that these words should be pronounced in normal talking fashion. The reader will need to decide for herself how "normally" one can pronounce "A CAT BATS AT A RAT" and how much a sentence of this type can be used to suggest variations in meaning. Nonetheless, Fries writes:

> The case for a very considerable amount of *properly directed and properly used oral reading from the very beginning* throughout the transfer stage and through this second stage of development rests primarily on the need to develop, along with the automatic responses to bundles of contrastive graphic shapes that actually are present in the writing, the ability to supply or produce the appropriate, or at least an appropriate, set of intonation and stress patterns that *fit* and display evidence of a total cumulative understanding.[25]

The question remains unanswered—How does one accomplish these admirable objectives with a sentence like BAT A FAT RAT? Is it possible that natural reading with appropriate pitch, stress, and so forth, will develop as the child acquires a more useful reading vocabulary? The differences between the reading vocabularies of linguistic materials and those more traditional are quite marked.

---

23. Ibid., p. 42. Italics not in original text.
24. Fries, *Linguistics and Reading,* p. 132.
25. Ibid., p. 207.

LeFevre's method, which he calls a "sentence" method in contrast to the "word" methods of Bloomfield, Barnhart, and Fries (sentence and word, as used here, refer to categories still within the linguistic framework, not the "sight" method previously described), places even more emphasis on oral reading. In a 1964 speech, LeFevre stated:

> Sensitivity to the nuances of language, appreciation of dialects, responsiveness to the forms of literature—all can best be cultivated on the basis of the whole sound of the piece when well read aloud. Not every reader need be an artist in oral interpretations—a producer; every child has his own potential, however, worthy of a little classroom attention.
>
> Surely every child should have many opportunities to hear and to attend to good oral interpretations of literature—to be a consumer. If the child has the authentic sound in his ear, his eye, then, in silent reading, can help his mental ear tune in on the mnemonic sound track by association with other pieces; but if he has never had the authentic sound in his ear, his mental ear will be deaf to the graphic presentation, no matter how beautifully done.[26]

Oral Reading as an Assessment Strategy

Most informal reading inventories and Goodman's *Miscue Analysis*[27] make extensive use of oral reading as one means of assessing a reader's (1) ability to apply word-attack or word-perception skills and (2) level or levels of comprehension. The process typically involves asking the reader to read aloud unfamiliar material, occasionally word lists,[28] but more frequently connected text. The teacher or examiner marks a copy of the text, using whatever coding system is required. Not infrequently, the performance is taped, making it possible to recheck for errors, corrected miscues, or other factors which may have been initially overlooked. Questioning regarding the content of the selection follows, and, occasionally, the reader is asked to retell the selection, in his own words, as a further check on comprehension. There is considerable controversy about the value of these assessment techniques,[29] and, clearly, whatever the values are must be viewed in terms of the time it takes to gather the data. Particularly with reference to miscue analysis, the writer shares Kenneth Goodman's position:

> A miscue, which we define as an actual observed response in oral reading which does not match the expected response, is like a window on the reading process.

---

26. Carl LeFevre, "A Comprehensive Linguistic Approach to Reading," *Elementary English* 42 (1965): 657. Used by permission of the National Council of Teachers of English and Carl A. LeFevre.

27. Kenneth Goodman, ed., *Miscue Analysis: Applications to Reading Instruction* (Urbana, Ill.: National Council of Teachers of English, 1973).

28. The reader is required to pronounce *live,* presented in list form, on one widely used inventory. Admittedly, the options have been reduced to two, and the verb form will probably be selected because it is more frequently used, but, even so, I question the need for such ambiguity!

29. Donald Shankweiler and Isabelle Liberman, "Misreading: A Search for Causes," in *Language by Ear and Eye: The Relationship Between Speech and Reading,* ed. James Kavanagh and Ignatius Mattingly (Cambridge, Mass.: M.I.T. Press, 1972), pp. 293–317.

Nothing the reader does in reading is accidental. Both his expected responses and his miscues are produced as he attempts to process the print and get to meaning. If we can understand how his miscues relate to the expected responses we can understand how he is using the reading process.[30]

Linguistics, Syllabication, and Reading

Of specific interest to reading teachers is the high level of current interest (among many linguists) in the value of syllabication as a reading skill. A *very* well known reading authority asked her graduate reading class, "after all, aren't morphemes and syllables the same thing?" As long as such ignorance is spread and as long as publishers search for *something* to teach third, fourth, and fifth graders, syllabication will probably continue to occupy a significant place on *some* publishers' lists of reading skills. Confusion continues to exist about the relationship between oral language and print, between morpheme and syllable. Dorothy Seymour concedes:

> Actually, the term syllabication itself is not a very apt one. The process might better be termed "word division for decoding" since the object is not to listen for syllables, or to count the number of syllables, but to decode the word by means of dividing into more recognizable visual parts. These parts may or may not represent the exact auditory syllables of the word as we believe we hear them. Thus, the important object is the decoding of the word, not the number of syllables in it.[31]

Seymour explains the confusion currently existing regarding the syllabic division of a word like *butter* (note Wardhaugh's reference to this issue, p. 30) as follows: "English has some digraphs made up of different letters (sh, ck) and others made up of the same letter (ss, tt). In both cases only one sound is signaled, not two."[32]

The position has been taken that only as much phonics should be taught as is necessary for purposes of promoting the beginning readers' independence in word attack/analysis/perception. A similar position is taken regarding the number of syllable-division generalizations taught. Typically, those taught are keyed to printer's conventions, not utterances; they are more basic to writing than to speaking.

Teachers are faced with the difficult task of explaining to children why contradictory generalizations are taught; for example, divide *butter* after the two *t*'s; between the two *t*'s. This dilemma may be resolved in the same way a similar problem with dictionary respellings might be; such ambiguities are the result of differing views of one language and how it is structured.

Linguistic Perspectives on Reading Comprehension

The arrangement of words in a sentence almost certainly affects the ease with which the meaning of the sentence can be comprehended. For example, passive sentences

---

30. Goodman, *Miscue Analysis*, p. 5.
31. Dorothy Seymour, "Word Division for Decoding," *The Reading Teacher* 27 (1973):276.
32. Ibid., p. 280. Cases like *accept* and *suggest* are difficult to handle using Seymour's generalization!

appear to be more difficult to comprehend than active sentences, and questions present more comprehension problems than statements. It seems that publishers are preparing materials for use in reading instruction which have moved some distance from the tightly controlled materials produced during the thirties, forties, and fifties, Levy's findings to the contrary.[33] Natural, speechlike language is stressed, and there is much less emphasis, even at primary levels, on controlling such factors as sentence length, and rate of introduction and repetition of new vocabulary. As a result, text material is probably much more interesting, and the selections in text-books and trade books are almost certainly more compatible. However, the pupil with serious, or even moderate, reading and/or language dialect problems, is likely to be quite discouraged when she encounters idiomatic speech, long and complicated sentences, and dialogue reflecting social or regional dialects. Is it possible to pro-duce materials for reading instruction which are neither vapid and insulting nor impossible to decode and comprehend? One would hope that language scholars, authors, publishers, and educators could accomplish this, each making a significant contribution.

Comprehension affects, and is affected by, phonological and morphological factors, and, as noted before, syntax also plays a role. The varied difficulty levels resulting from active-passive and statement-question transformations have already been noted. Comprehension is also affected by the position of a word in a sentence and whether a proper noun or its pronoun substitute is selected. The distance of a pronoun from its referent is a significant factor in comprehension, as are the number of embeddings. Certain conjunctions cause much more difficulty than others—*because* and *although* are not understood, or decoded with comprehension, as easily as *and* and *or*.[34]

What does this mean? Should teachers avoid using materials which may be difficult to comprehend? Not if there are compensating factors! Even pupils with moderate to severe reading problems will attempt to decode and comprehend ma-terial which is of high interest. One implication seems clear: a teacher who is *aware* of some potential language barriers to comprehension can help pupils antici-pate the problem and solve it before it occurs. Obviously prediction, anticipating what word or phrase will come next, is an important part of the reading act, for mature readers particularly. Skillful teachers can help children win what Goodman calls a "psycholinguistic guessing game."[35] It should be clear by now that psycho-linguists, in particular, are deeply involved in studying comprehension and do *not* view *thinking* or responding to language as beyond their area or areas of concern and expertise.

Because the issue of readability and how it is to be measured involves all of the strands or components of language identified previously, brief consideration will be given to the topic of readability in general and to cloze technique in particular.

---

33. Beatrice Levy, "The Oral Language of First Graders Compared to the Language of Beginning Reading Texts," in *Black Dialects and Reading,* ed. Bernice Cullinan (Urbana, Ill.: National Council of Teachers of English, 1974), pp. 29–40.

34. William Fagan, "Transformations and Comprehension," *The Reading Teacher* 25 (1972): 169–72.

35. Kenneth Goodman, "Reading: A Psycholinguistic Guessing Game," *Journal of the Reading Specialist* 6 (1967):126–35.

Readability is defined as the sum of factors, and the interactive effect of these factors, which determine an individual's ability to comprehend what he reads. In the very thorough annotated bibliography dealing with comprehension compiled for the International Reading Association, Green notes that none of the readability formulas in use today take "adequate account of style, symbolism, concept density, or quality of a work."[36] It might be added that neither do such formulas take into account sentence complexity. However, Green may have included this in his general term *style*.

Factors typically considered in determining readability are number of words in a sentence, number of syllables in a word and, frequently, an analytical comparison of words in a selection with words included on a standardized list of some type. Of the most widely used formulas, the Lorge formula is identified by Chall as most appropriate for young children,[37] although the Spache is the most widely used. The Dale-Chall is identified as best for materials written for older children and adults. The SMOG and Fry are recent additions to the list of readability formulas, and they have the advantages of being both reasonably predictive (when compared with the more complex formulas) and quite easy to apply.

The cloze technique or procedure was developed by Taylor, and reported by him in 1953.[38] Comprehension difficulty and, some would say, readability, is estimated by the random or patterned deletion of words from passages. Subjects are asked to fill in the blanks with the exact words deleted. The difficulty rating for a passage is determined by counting the number and computing the percentage of blanks filled in with precisely the same word used by the original writer. It has been suggested that a 75 percent criterion be considered adequate for the so-called instructional level and 90 percent for the independent level.

It may be true that cloze tests do not constitute a readability formula in the narrowest definition of that term, but they do have the advantage of taking into account the total linguistic structure of a selection in contrast to other widely used formulas. The cloze technique provides a tool which may be used by the classroom teacher to assess the difficulty of a passage. The findings of Bormuth suggest that it is an effective measure of pupils' comprehension.[39]

Vocabularies in Linguistic Reading Materials

Look, come, see, oh, and so forth, are frequently included at the beginning levels in standard texts. Linguists tell us that words such as these lead only to confusion—and it is no wonder that they have to be memorized. Words such as *look* and *see* are confusing when presented in close proximity because the double vowel in *see*

36. Richard Green, *Comprehension in Reading: An Annotated Bibliography* (Newark, Del.: International Reading Association, 1971).

37. Jean Chall, "Readability: An Appraisal of Research and Application," *Educational Research Monograph* (Columbus, Ohio: The Ohio State University), 1958.

38. Wilson Taylor, "Cloze Procedure: A New Tool for Measuring Readability," *Journalism Quarterly* 30 (1953):415–33.

39. John Bormuth, "Cloze as a Measure of Readability," in *International Reading Association, Conference Proceedings,* vol. 8 (Newark, Del.: International Reading Association, 1963), pp. 131–34.

produces a long[40] vowel sound; the double vowel in *look* does not. Words like *come* and *home* lead to confusion because one word supports the rule which states that the vowel preceding the silent *e* is long, while the other word violates, or represents an exception to, the same rule. Linguists, then, propose reading vocabularies, at the beginning levels, which follow a basic pattern of consonant-vowel-consonant, with the medial vowel always short, this vowel sound being more frequent and less subject to regional variations. The first story of *Frog Fun,* it should be noted, introduces *Pud, Zip,* and *hop* at the earliest levels.[41] Of the twenty-three words of the first preprimer, only one, *little,* is a two-syllable word. Two words, *jump* and *pond,* end with blends. The rest follow the C-V-C pattern, and no long vowels are presented until Book Two, *Tuggy.* The long *e* sound is presented, and reinforced in *see, sees, sleep,* and *sleeps.* An interesting variation is presented when *slips* follows *sleeps.* It is presumed by the time the child reaches this stage (Book 2) such a phonemic substitution will not cause any problem.[42]

Bloomfield and Barnhart also use the C-V-C pattern and emphasize the short vowel sound throughout the first thirty-six lessons. It has already been pointed out that Bloomfield and Barnhart do not object to the use of nonsense syllables (vad, rad, ap, ag), claiming that these same syllables are parts of some words and so will have later utility. In *Let's Read,* a fairly regular pattern is followed: short *a* (*man*), short *i* (*pin*), short *u* (*rug*), short *e* (*pet*), and finally short *o* (*pop*), with the vowel always placed between two consonants; the child's reading vocabulary is limited to one-syllable words for the first thirty-six lessons. The first two-syllable words are compound words (*milkman, himself*), which present only minor stress problems and which use short vowel sounds.[43]

The McGraw-Hill programmed linguistic material for beginning reading is similar to the programs described above, but *man* (which follows the C-V-C pattern) and *ant* (which does not) are presented in the same lesson. Children are introduced to these two words and then asked to complete blanks placed beside appropriate or inappropriate pictures.

an ant.

Am I an ant? (Yes, No)   Am I a man? (Yes, No)   I am

a man.[44]

Children are expected to select correct responses and to check the correctness of responses by removing the strip of paper that covers the answer key on each page.

---

40. Ronald Wardhaugh's discussion of this terminology problem might interest the reader. Venezky has also indicated support for terms such as *checked* and *open.* Some of the newer reading materials include *unglided* (short) and *glided* (long). I have attempted for some time to encourage publishers, writers, and teachers to discontinue the use of the terms *long* and *short;* they are, at the least, inaccurate and misleading. However, presumably because they communicate, they continue to be used and will be used in this chapter.

41. Clara Stratemeyer and Henry Smith, Jr., *Frog Fun,* The Linguistic Science Readers (Evanston, Ill.: Harper & Row, 1965), pp. 6–8.

42. Clara Stratemeyer and Henry Smith, Jr., *Tuggy,* The Linguistic Science Readers (Evanston, Ill.: Harper & Row, 1963).

43. Bloomfield and Barnhart, *Let's Read,* p. 139.

44. From *Programmed Reading, Book 1,* by Sullivan Associates. Copyright © 1963 by Sullivan Associates. Published by McGraw-Hill.

Although not specifically related to vocabulary, the problem of sentence structure should be discussed. One publisher, in particular, has borne the brunt of many jokes and has been ridiculed for the use of unchildlike sentences. The story of the first-grade teacher who exclaimed, following an automobile accident, "Oh! Oh! Oh! Look! Look! Look! Damn! Damn! Damn!" illustrates, in a colorful and amusing fashion, the point to be made here. Ruth Strickland,[45] Walter Loban,[46] and others have gathered abundant evidence that children do *not* talk in preprimerese. They begin school using many sentence types easily, and with some sophistication in varying these types to make their conversation interesting. If our first-grade teacher gave evidence of retardation in her speech patterns, under stress, how much more harm is done to young children when they attempt to transfer what they already know about talking to reading. It is worth noting here that there appears to be a high, positive correlation between children's ability to use a variety of sentence types in their speech and their ability to read.

Linguists have already made an impact in the area of sentence structure in children's reading materials. The major publishers now include contractions at quite an early stage, and a variety of sentence types appear much sooner in recently revised materials than in earlier editions. This is certainly an encouraging step, and the result should be reading materials which are much more lifelike and interesting for children and their teachers.

Contrasts Between Linguistic Reading Materials and Materials of a More Traditional Nature

At this point, it would be wise to summarize, and to provide a condensed statement of, the major differences between the newer linguistic materials and more traditional texts. The reader must keep in mind, however, that *the* (with a long *e*) linguistic approach does not exist and probably never will. Linguists disagree about many basic points, and their materials vary in many significant respects. However, there are important contrasts between the typical and well-accepted, basal reading materials of the past and the newer materials which claim to be linguistically sound.

It should be stressed that, in the foreseeable future, most major publishers will market materials which show the results of influence by linguists. In order to gain acceptance in the 1970s and 1980s, a basal reading series will almost certainly include at *least* one linguistic consultant, along with a list of authors who are teachers, psychologists, clinicians, and/or teacher educators. Several reputable linguists are authors who have prepared materials either for pupils, teachers, or both. Many of the marked contrasts between linguistic and nonlinguistic materials discussed in this chapter will no longer be so marked. This is already true of the revised materials published by several of the largest and most important contributors to the school textbook field.

---

45. Ruth Strickland, *The Language of Elementary School Children: Its Relationship to the Language of Reading Textbooks and the Quality of Reading of Selected Children*, Indiana University Bulletin of the School of Education, vol. 38, no. 4 (Bloomington, 1962).

46. Walter Loban, *The Language of Elementary School Children*, National Council of Teachers of English Research Report no. 1 (Champaign, Ill.: 1963).

The following areas probably represent the most significant areas of contrast at the present time:

1. *Definitions of the reading process.* Linguists insist that we have confused the reading process with the *use* of what is read, that meaning is not exclusively the province of interpreting printed symbols, and that reading is in essence a process of transferring what the child already knows about speech and auditory signals to reading. This results in much less concern for meaningful content at the beginning reading stage. Bloomfield and Barnhart even sanction the use of nonsense syllables, but Fries, Smith, and other linguists, who have proposed significant changes in the content of beginning reading programs, do not.

2. *The alphabet and beginning reading.* Linguists are in general agreement that the child should be able to recognize the letters of the alphabet and to associate a sound with each letter prior to beginning reading. Bloomfield seems to be alone in insisting that children *name* each letter—aye, be, see, and so forth. In some traditional basal programs children learn the alphabet in a more incidental manner, and knowledge of the alphabet is not considered crucial to success in beginning reading.

3. *Content of beginning reading programs.* Almost all the programs prepared so far concentrate on words (except for *a* and *the* which are necessary for making a "complete sentence") which follow a fairly consistent pattern of consonant-vowel-consonant (*bag-big-bug*, etc.).

4. *Use of pictures.* Linguistic programs vary in the extent to which pictures are used, but many linguistic reading specialists avoid including pictures which aid in interpreting the text. In linguistic materials, if they are included at all, pictures are frequently oblique or abstract and, although attractive, do nothing to add to the story in a content sense. Bloomfield and Barnhart include no pictures at all, and the last pages of the final story in the Harper and Row preprimers are without illustrations.

5. *Implications of linguistics for middle- and upper-grade reading programs.* Linguists have concentrated their efforts almost entirely at the beginning level, since they claim that success at this level enables the child to read any material with ease later on. The one consistent piece of advice given by linguists for middle- and upper-grade reading is that materials of high literary quality be included. LeFevre places unusual stress upon literature as a vehicle for enabling children to understand better the form and structure of their language. Most linguists agree that the carefully controlled vocabularies in current basal reading programs have caused such materials to be somewhat deficient in literary quality. It is as though some linguists were saying, "Let us work with admittedly uninteresting patterns at first, since it will free children sooner to read that which is worth reading. Motivation? This comes through the child's knowledge of the progress he's making!"

6. *Intonation and oral reading.* There appears to be a general trend toward more emphasis on oral reading in reading programs of all kinds, but linguists, with the emphasis they place on the primacy of speech, could be expected to give a major role to oral reading, and they do. There is disagreement concern-

ing the wisdom of calling the letter names of the alphabet, and Fries would have children recognize the visual patterns first, but all agree that reading aloud serves to reinforce the relationship of the spoken word (or sentence) to the written symbol, a relationship they consider vital. Existing linguistic materials, however, are not easily read with interesting stress, pitch, and so forth. (Pat a fat cat.)

7. *Sentence structure.* Linguists are open to criticism here, and they have received some, because their advice regarding using a variety of sentence patterns and a more natural way of having characters speak has been violated in the children's materials they have prepared. A question asked earlier bears repeating—is "Nan can fan Dan" a more interesting sentence than "Dick can see Jane"? However, linguists' emphasis upon a strong literary basis for reading instruction in the middle and upper grades suggests that their belief in intonation as an important meaning-bearing vehicle is sincere. Linguists have very little to say, incidentally, about problems related to reading in science, mathematics, or any of the content fields for that matter. It is assumed that this is a problem for the practitioner.

Implications for Today's and Tomorrow's Reading Programs

Understanding the linguists' approaches to reading instruction and sampling their materials are of interest to the professional, but do the linguists' recommendations make any sense? Are they practical? Are any of them worth incorporating into curricula for tomorrow's reading? For next fall? Must an entire "linguistic" program be bought, or can some basic premises be made part of the language arts programs of teachers using materials they now have, but using more sophisticated and knowledgeable methods?

The results the linguists claim to have achieved through the use of their materials suggest that the approaches they recommend are highly successful, particularly with "culturally disadvantaged" children and with children who have tried to learn to read for several years without success. Although most linguists admit their programs are not panaceas, claims to the contrary are occasionally made on behalf of such programs.

What can the classroom teacher glean from linguistic programs which will enrich and enhance her teaching and her pupils' learning? The answer to this question might be approached through restating some basic linguistic principles.

1. *Oral language development is basic to the development of reading skills.* Knowing this, the classroom teacher will provide many opportunities for the child to dictate stories and reports to be recorded on experience charts. A tape recorder is a very valuable device to use with experience charts—what better reinforcement: "This is what I said—this is the way what I said is written!" Pictures can be labeled, and a group of pictures with similar labels can be collected to make a book, a *book* to be *read* by its authors and others as well.

   Plans, assignments, and schedules can be discussed, then recorded for future reference. Teachers can guide children to the discovery of similar sound patterns and their written representations. Sentence structure, the roles of pitch, stress, and juncture—all can be taught, or reviewed and reinforced, by the extensive use of the tape recorder and experience chart records.

2. *Common spelling patterns form a useful basis for a beginning reading vocabulary.* The examples of the content of the beginning reading materials referred to thus far as linguistic would seem to have limited appeal to most children. They may be useful as a basis for exercises designed to help the child achieve independence in word analysis. For example, instead of including a sentence such as "Pat a fat cat" in beginning reading materials, why not develop the concept involved as a pattern, letting children suggest as lengthy a list of words following this pattern as possible. The C-V-C pattern is a common pattern and a useful one, but it does not lend itself to a variety of sentences appropriate for intonation. The use of compound words as the first two-syllable words is probably an effective technique, since the problem of which syllable is stressed does not occur or is not quite so important for meaning-bearing purposes. Again, work with compound words of this type could precede and/or supplement the utilization of words of this type in context.

3. *If pitch, stress, and pause, or juncture, are important in conveying meaning in speech, they are important in oral reading.* It would seem that, for purposes of getting the author's meaning, silent reading should precede oral reading (although Bloomfield would disagree with this concept). Then, through discussion of the author's purposes and the character's motivation, excerpts of dialogue from the selection could be read aloud, as the character might say them. If there is disagreement, so much the better; then stress, pitch, and the whole gamut of devices we use in speech to convey meaning could be summoned to support each position.

Prior to the stage at which children can interpret materials in such a sophisticated manner, they can try changing meaning by repeating certain ordinary phrases:

> Why did you come to the party?
> Do you like that book?
> What did you do in school today?

The list could be much longer. The point is, even young children can soon see that the question *"When* did you come to the party?" is not the same question at all as "When did *you* come to the party?" A sensitive teacher can use elements of children's speech to develop this same kind of understanding: "I heard Sue say this in the hall this morning; how would she have said it if she had meant . . .?" As children dictate stories to the teacher or bring compositions to the teacher for "editorial help," the emphasis, again, should be on meaning: "Wouldn't it be better to arrange your sentence so the important part comes first? How could you do this?"

The literature program, especially the poetry program, is tremendously important in helping children see the relationship between sentence structure and meaning. There is a risk that selections might be overanalyzed, but it may be a risk worth taking in order to discuss how a character might really have said this, or how our voices should be used to make important the words the poet wanted to be important.

Phonics and Linguistics

Linguists are almost unanimous in condemning the practice of calling sounds in isolation, whether consonants or vowels. Sounds do not exist, in any meaningful sense, apart from a given word in which they combine to express an idea. The extreme of this position would be that words do not exist in isolation apart from sentences; "sentences make words, words do not make sentences" is an over-simplification of a linguistic maxim. There is no desire to go this far—the problems connected with isolated letter-sound drill must be dealt with first!

The practice of having children first isolate and then blend sounds to make words is, at the very least, unnatural and can contribute little or nothing to meaningful reading. The linguists quoted in this chapter, without exception, oppose this practice and state categorically that the *word* is the very smallest meaning-bearing unit with which children should work. There are ample quotations to support this statement throughout the chapter, and none will be repeated here.

Similar sound patterns, formed by similar patterns of letters, can be profitably identified by children and can be a vehicle leading to greater independence in word analysis. The practice of calling isolated, meaningless letter names or sounds these letter names infrequently represent probably has little value as part of a program designed to help children learn to read.

Elementary Teachers and Knowledge of Their Language

A book such as this can only make a small beginning in helping an elementary teacher acquire essential knowledge about the language she uses so glibly and, too often, without much understanding. The ultimate solution to the problem of *how much* linguistics to include in a reading program rests with the elementary teacher. A teacher can include in her reading program only such elements of linguistic understanding as she possesses. The readings suggested in the Selected References at the conclusion of the chapter can help the teacher develop some of the most basic understandings which are essential to a more language-centered or linguistic reading program.

Summary

In recent years, recommendations of linguists have been added to the recommenda-tions of others who advocate change and reform of traditional reading methods in the elementary schools of the United States. It was pointed out that linguists are scholars, students of our language, but not, ordinarily, professional educators. Nevertheless, because of their depth of understanding of language and because reading is a language-centered process, the reading programs developed by linguists deserve to be examined objectively, and appropriate elements of linguistic programs should be put into classroom practice. The majority of these programs have not been tried on a large scale, and final judgment probably should be withheld pending such trial and more adequate research regarding the success of the programs with children whose backgrounds, personalities, interests, and intellectual capacities differ.

A brief historical analysis of reading instruction in the United States was included. The rise and decline of various phonics methods was stressed, as was that of the word method. It was pointed out that in recent years the term most appropriately applied to reading methods is *eclectic,* suggesting that superior teachers, at least, rely upon a variety of methods and techniques, not on phonics or the sight method exclusively.

An effort was made to contrast several of the more popular linguistic reading programs with reading programs which have been popular in the recent past. Most reading programs claim to be linguistically sound, and most publishers have secured the services of a linguist as an author or as a consultant. It is no longer a matter of linguistics or not, but *whose* linguistics, and how much of it, to include in a given reading program.

The point was made that the most basic differences between linguistic programs and those which teachers have grown accustomed to using lies in the definition of the reading process. Whereas reading has been traditionally defined in very broad terms, including perception, comprehension, utilization and/or application of reading skills and content, linguists insist that reading is essentially a process of transferring what the child already knows about speech to the interpretation of the written word. They recommend that throughout the reading process, especially in its beginning stages, the child's attention be drawn to the relationships between speech and writing.

Most linguists advocate helping the child acquire some knowledge of the alphabet. There is some controversy about the importance of being able to "call" the letters, but there is general agreement that children should learn the alphabetic principle—that one letter may stand for one or several sounds.

It is reasonable to expect that many linguists, with their stress on the primacy of speech, would be strong advocates of oral reading. Because they are aware of the importance of intonation in encoding and decoding—in conveying meaning— linguists want oral reading to be an integral part of reading programs. It has been suggested that materials developed by linguists make this advice somewhat difficult to follow.

The vocabulary of beginning reading materials follows a definite pattern and varies little from one linguistic program to another. The first words, whether presented in isolation or in stories, are usually one-syllable words following a consonant-vowel-consonant pattern. This appears to be a contradiction to the linguists' recommendations regarding the use of varied and interesting sentence patterns and the inclusion of sentences which lend themselves to a variety of intonation patterns. When forced to choose, linguists generally choose the regularity of spelling pattern first, hoping that the other goals will be achieved later.

It follows from their definitions of reading that linguists do not place much emphasis on meaning at the beginning stages; "Pat a fat cat" and "Nan can fan Dan" may be considered something less than rich and fruitful sentences! Illustrations are of minimal importance, serving perhaps to attract, to intrigue, but never to tell the story.

The chapter concluded with some general suggestions for classroom teachers:

1. Make full use of tape recordings of children's speech; relate this to experience charts, reports, and so forth.
2. A rich and selective literature program can help to teach children about the structure of their language.
3. Oral reading probably deserves more emphasis than it has received in recent years. Ordinarily (except for diagnostic purposes) oral reading should *follow* silent reading, for the sake of better comprehension of typical reading material.
4. The C-V-C pattern is a helpful one for beginners, but could be worked on as a complement to materials which are better for purposes of utilizing interesting sentence patterns and teaching recognition of the role of intonation in conveying meaning.
5. Teachers need to deepen and broaden their understanding of the language they use every day in order to help children understand this language, spoken and written, as thoroughly as possible.

Selected References

Allen, Robert. "Better Reading Through the Recognition of Grammatical Relations." *The Reading Teacher* 18 (1964): 194–98.

Baratz, Joan, and Roger Shuy, eds. *Teaching Black Children to Read*. Washington, D.C.: Center for Applied Linguistics, 1969.

Beaver, Joseph. "Transformational Grammar and the Teaching of Reading." *Research in the Teaching of English* 2 (1968): 161–71.

Bloomfield, Leonard, and Clarence Barnhart. *Let's Read: A Linguistic Approach*. Detroit: Wayne State University Press, 1961.

Durkin, Dolores. *Phonics, Linguistics and Reading*. New York: Teachers College Press, Bureau of Publications, Columbia University, 1972.

Fries, Charles. *Linguistics and Reading*. New York: Holt, Rinehart & Winston, 1963.

Gibson, Eleanor, and Harry Levin. "Linguistic Concepts Necessary to Study Reading." In *The Psychology of Reading*. Cambridge, Mass.: M.T.T. Press, 1975.

Goodman, Kenneth, ed. *Miscue Analysis: Applications to Reading Instruction*. Urbana, Ill.: National Council of Teachers of English, 1973.

_____. *The Psycholinguistic Nature of the Reading Process*. Detroit: Wayne State University Press, 1969.

————, and James Fleming, eds. *Psycholinguistics and the Teaching of Reading.* Newark, Del.: International Reading Association, 1968.

Gove, Philip. "Reading from the Lexicographer's Viewpoint." *The Reading Teacher* 18 (1964): 199–201.

Heilman, Arthur. *Phonics in Proper Perspective.* 3rd ed. Columbus, Ohio: Charles E. Merrill Publishing Co., 1976.

Hunt, Barbara. "Black Dialect and Third and Fourth Graders' Performance on the Gray Oral Reading Test." *Reading Research Quarterly* 10 (1974–75): 103–24.

Kane, Robert, Mary Byrne, and Mary Hater. *Helping Children Read Mathematics.* New York: American Book Co., 1974.

Kavanagh, James, and Ignatius Mattingly, eds. *Language by Ear and Eye: The Relationship Between Speech and Reading.* Cambridge, Mass.: M.I.T. Press, 1972.

Kerfoot, James, ed. and comp. *First Grade Reading Programs.* Newark, Del.: International Reading Association, 1965.

Levin, Harry, and Joanna Williams, eds. *Basic Studies in Reading.* New York: Basic Books, 1970).

McDavid, Raven. "Dialectology and the Teaching of Reading." *The Reading Teacher* 18 (1964): 206–13.

Miller, John. "Linguistics and Comprehension." *Elementary English* 51 (1974): 853–54.

Rode, Sara. "Development of Phrase and Clause Boundary Reading in Children." *Reading Research Quarterly* 10(1): 124–42.

Ruddell, Robert. *Reading-Language Instruction, Innovative Practices.* Englewood Cliffs, N.J.: Prentice-Hall, 1974.

Sticht, Thomas, Lawrence Beck, Robert Hauke, Glenn Klerman, and James James. *Auding and Reading: A Developmental Model.* Alexandria, Va.: Human Resources Research Organization, 1974.

Strickland, Ruth. *The Contribution of Structural Linguistics to the Teaching of Reading, Writing and Grammar in the Elementary School.* Bloomington, Ind.: Bureau of Educational Studies and Teaching, Indiana University, 1963.

3

Linguistics and the Teaching of Spelling

It has been noted that many linguists believe that beginning reading programs should involve acquainting the child with a sequence of phoneme-grapheme correspondences. The fact that our language permits us to use only twenty-six letters to represent as many as forty-eight significant sound units has serious and far reaching implications for spelling programs as well as reading programs.

Hanna et al. note:

Since the American English orthography traditionally has been conceived to have little correspondence with the spoken language, spelling words must be selected and grouped on some basis other than the alphabetic principle underlying the orthography. . . .

Typically, weekly spelling lessons have been built around a list of about 10 to 20 words that may be classified in different ways:

1. Words grouped at random (e.g., *tree, fine, sick*)

2. Words grouped according to visual similarities (e.g., *nation, function, invitation*)

3. Words grouped about a spelling rule or generalization (e.g., words that end in y, change the y to i before adding suffixes, or the es of the plural form)

4. Words grouped into meaningful association around a typical child interest (playing with dolls) or a curricular topic (colonial life)

51

5. Words grouped in phonemic families (e.g., long *a* sound as in *make, made,* spelled a and a final silent e.)[1]

Other considerations in selecting words for spelling lists included frequency and commonness of use and the words' significance and levels of difficulty.

With reference to methodology, Hanna et al. conclude: "In sum, a fundamental assumption regarding the teaching and learning of spelling, from a traditional point of view, has been a heavy reliance upon visual learning."[2]

Part of the spelling problem, and there is serious disagreement concerning how large a part, is undoubtedly due to inconsistencies in phoneme-grapheme correspondences in American English. Clarence Barnhart claims that there are over 230 spellings for about 40 basic sounds. He notes: "The letters of the alphabet are directions to say the sounds, but about 25 percent of the time the English alphabet fails or misleads us in giving directions on the pronunciation of words."[3]

Hanna, Hodges, and Hanna report the results of a study conducted at Stanford University in which a 3,000 word vocabulary was analyzed in terms of phoneme-grapheme correspondences. They write:

This 1951 research study indicated that the American English language has a surprising amount of consistency in its graphemic representation of speech sounds. Here are some findings:

1. Roughly four-fifths of the phonemes contained in the words comprising the traditional spelling vocabulary of the elementary school child approximate the alphabetic principle in their letter representations.

2 Approximately one-fifth of the phonemes contained in the words comprising that spelling vocabulary deviate substantially from the alphabetic principle in their letter representations.

3. Nearly three-fourths of the vowel phonemes do not represent significant spelling problems, since they have a consistent letter representation from about 57 percent to about 99 percent of the times they occur.

4. About 82 percent of the consonant clusters have only one spelling.

5. Single-consonant phonemes are represented by consistent spellings about nine-tenths of the time they occur.

The results of this study indicated that our written code is not so inconsistent that analysis of phoneme-grapheme correspondences cannot provide the basis for teaching spelling. In short, spelling curriculum specialists had overlooked the most important feature of our written language—that it is alphabetically based—and had failed to recognize the importance of developing the sound-to-letter concept.[4]

As noted, the degree of correspondence between sound and letter in American English is a matter of controversy and is of some consequence to those concerned with spelling programs and instructional procedures.

---

1. Paul Hanna et al., *Phoneme-Grapheme Correspondence as Cues to Spelling Improvement* (Washington, D.C.: U.S. Dept. of Health, Education, and Welfare, U.S. Office of Education, 1967), p. 7.

2. Ibid., p. 8.

3. Clarence Barnhart, "Establishing and Maintaining Standard Patterns of Speech," in *Readings in Applied English Linguistics,* ed. Harold Allen (New York: Appleton-Century-Crofts, 1958), p. 378.

4. Paul Hanna, Richard Hodges, and Jean Hanna, *Spelling: Structure and Strategies* (Boston: Houghton Mifflin Co., 1971), p. 76.

Project 1991

It is frustrating for this writer to be forced to summarize the results of a study as massive, and with such significance to educators as well as linguists, as Project 1991. The interested reader will almost certainly want to obtain additional information from the appropriate end-of-chapter references. This study was conducted at Stanford University under the general direction of Paul Hanna, and the final report was published in 1966, written by Paul Hanna, Jean Hanna, Richard Hodges, and Hugh Rudorf. The study involved the computer analysis of over 17,000 words, with the purpose of studying phoneme-grapheme correspondences under various conditions. It was found that the great majority of consonants had single spellings which were used 80 percent or more of the time; only a handful of vowel sounds had single spellings which occurred with such high frequency. Further, the analysis disclosed that many phonemes have quite predictable spellings in certain positions; the position of phonemes directly influences their spelling. There was less clear-cut evidence concerning the effect of stress, although this factor must also be taken into account in studying a word. Hanna, Hodges, and Hanna write:

> The Stanford study we have been summarizing pointed up the basically alphabetic nature of American-English spelling. It showed that, contrary to traditional viewpoints, the orthography is far from erratic. It is based upon relationships between phonemes and graphemes—relationships that are sometimes complex in nature but which, when clarified, demonstrate that American-English orthography, like that of other languages, is largely systematic.[5]

In Phase II of the project, the computer was asked to spell the 17,000+ words, using spelling principles based on the findings from Phase I regarding phoneme-grapheme relationships. Using these principles, the computer spelled half of the words without error, and an additional 37 percent with only one error. These errors occurred in compound words, and also because the computer was not programmed to double the spellings of certain consonants. Further, certain borrowed words retained their original spellings and the computer applied principles related to American English. Only about 3 percent of the words were classified as *mavericks* —words which do not conform to the principles applied to the basic vocabulary used in the study. The findings of Project 1991 clearly indicate the need for spelling programs that emphasize the consistent relationship between sounds and letters. Programs of this type will help pupils achieve earlier independence in spelling and free them from the rote memorization which has been so prevalent in our instructional practices.

Causes of the Spelling "Dilemma"

The Hannas write:

> Today we assume that the letters of the alphabet originally represented single sounds and that the first attempts to write a word consisted of writing a letter symbol

---

5. Ibid., p. 83.

54

for each sound heard in a word. Each successive writing of the word was either a direct copy of the original or an independent phonemic (indivisible sound unit) analysis and transcription or an embellished spelling of the original. Printers, in particular, in the absence of other authority, assumed the role of arbiters of orthography. The whimsy of the printers added to the already complicated problem of spelling and was restrained only with the advent of the dictionary.

Thanks to the English dictionary, spelling is, today, fairly well standardized. But the schools are still struggling with the problem of how best to teach pupils this standardized spelling of our language. Pupils and teachers continue to be harassed by the "phonetically unreliable" structure of English and hounded by the public which demands an improvement in spelling ability and performance.[6]

Change in pronunciation is surely one cause of our present spelling dilemma. A reader of Chaucer's *Canterbury Tales* (assuming such a reader is skilled in historic linguistics) pronounces "wyf" (wife) as \wēf\; "lyf" (life) as \lēf\; and "knight" as \knĭgt\. Pronunciation changed, but, in many cases, the spelling or the graphic representation of the pronunciation did not.

It is not news to the reader that English is a hybrid language. It has been enriched by the addition of words from French (*realm, crown, state, power, enemy*), Italian (*balcony, cornice, corridor, pistol*), and Spanish (*cafeteria, escapade, banana*). Because the phoneme-grapheme relationships in other languages are not the same as they are in English, many of these borrowed words do not "fit" or are not spelled as one might expect them to be spelled. They do not fit any of our basic English spelling patterns.

Finally, we might list as a third basic cause of our spelling dilemma the ineptitude of the printers, editors, and proofreaders who supervised the production of books and reference books during the period immediately following the development of movable type and the printing press. It might be noted that many of these printers were Dutch, and thus they tended to impose Dutch spellings on English. Printers frequently practiced creative spelling; they were not particularly well educated, and undetected errors were all too often reproduced until they became standardized and generally accepted as correct.

To summarize: although there is widespread disagreement regarding the *extent* of phoneme-grapheme discrepancy which exists in English, it seems clear that there are some words, in common usage, which no not fit standard English spelling patterns and must be learned by memorization without real understanding. Three causes for this inconsistency have been suggested:

1. Changes occurred in the pronunciation of words which were not accompanied by appropriate or consistent changes in the way these words were spelled.
2. Words were borrowed from other languages. These words may follow consistent spelling patterns for the languages from which they were borrowed, but not for English.
3. Correct spelling was not a serious problem until printed material gained relatively wide circulation. Printers exercised much control over the standardization of the written symbols of a language which previously had not been

6. Jean and Paul Hanna, "Spelling as a School Subject: A Brief History," *The National Elementary School Principal* 38 (1959): 8.

frequently put in writing. Printers, copy editors, and proofreaders used their own judgment regarding the "proper" spelling of a word, and this judgment was often without much foundation in the literate skills. Today, correct spelling is one of the hallmarks of the educated person. It should be kept in mind that this has not always been so.

The Child's Acquisition of Generalizations Regarding Phoneme-Grapheme Correspondences

Charles Read has conducted interesting and highly significant studies of the manner in which young children represent the sounds they already know with letters. These studies were conducted informally, and much of the data has not been subjected to empirical analysis. Nevertheless, there is clear evidence that speech sounds are categorized in ways which make sense to children, and, further, it is a mistake for first- and second-grade teachers to assume that pupils make only random and naive assumptions in this area:

Read reports:

> The children tended to represent the potentially syllabic consonants [r, l, m, n] and [ŋ] without a preceding vowel . . . a second special case is that of the affricated [t] that occurs before [r] in English, as in truck. . . . The third special case is that of preconsonantal nasals, such as the [n] of want, which the children strongly tended to omit in spelling.[7]

Specifically, Read found that the preschoolers and primary grade pupils he studied rather consistently spelled *pen* without a vowel letter at all or with an *a*, *truck* was spelled *chrak*, and *sank* was spelled *sak*. This represents a major oversimplification of the findings, and the reader is particularly urged to read the monograph in which Read's research is reported. His comments on the educational significance of his findings are especially pertinent:

> The educational importance of invented spelling and phonetic categorization by children is that we cannot assume that a child must approach reading and writing as an untrained animal approaches a maze—with no discernible prior conception of its structure. Evidently a child may come to school with a knowledge of some phonological categories and relations; without conscious awareness, the child may seek to relate English spelling to those relations in some generally systematic way. If this inference is correct, some long neglected questions become crucial for understanding and facilitating the process of learning to read and write: What levels of phonological analysis do children tacitly control at various stages of development? How do these analyses relate to lexical representations and to standard spelling? How can literacy instruction build on this relationship while encouraging children to extend and deepen their notion of the sound system of the language?
>
> The invented spelling and our consequent experiments do not show precisely

---

7. Charles Read, *Children's Categorization of Speech Sounds in English* (Urbana, Ill.: National Council of Teachers of English, 1975), p. 14.

what constitutes an optimal orthography, nor do they resolve all the theoretical issues here. But they do suggest that the picture is . . . complex: children analyze and categorize phones according to certain phonetic characteristics, and in some circumstances, they may assign spellings to these categories, rather than to individual phonemes.[8]

It seems clear that the classroom teacher must exhibit concern for the linguistic bases of an effective spelling program, operating on the best available current data about the structure of our language, and, as Read suggests, must also take into account the evidence regarding children's acquisition of generalizations related to correspondences between sound units and letter units.

Selection of Words in Spelling Programs

There has been much discussion, over a period of years, concerning the importance of "interest," "motivation," and "words children need for current writing" in determining which words to include in graded spelling lists. There is neither the space, nor would it be appropriate, to give a thorough review of instructional programs in spelling and the changes that have occurred in the teaching of spelling through the years. The reader is almost certainly familiar with Noah Webster's famous *Blue-Back Speller* and its preeminent role as a reader as well as a speller for many years.

With all the evident concern for a consistent "phonetic" or "phonic" approach to spelling programs, from Webster's day to the present, the words selected for study and emphasis at various grade levels have been remarkably inconsistent. It appears that authors of spelling series have tried to achieve two rather incompatible and almost dichotomous objectives at the same time. They have selected words with reference to areas which receive curricular emphasis at specific grade levels (for example, "Community Helpers" in the second grade). A second criterion has been utility. What words do children use in their "personal" and "practical" writing (to borrow Alvina Burrows's terms)? What words are stressed in the basal reading programs? If these questions can be answered satisfactorily, then the spelling list we provide for children should have strong motivation "built in." This sounds much simpler than it is in actual practice. *If* the same vocabulary studies were used as basic, *if* even a majority of children came from very similar socioeconomic backgrounds with a predictable core of preschool experiences upon which to build, and *if* elementary school curricula in the United States were standardized, then some uniformity could be expected. Because all second graders do not study community helpers, because rural children bring to school a somewhat different core of experiences than inner-city urban children, and because students of children's vocabularies have not used similar research techniques, we have almost no consistency at all in the words found in graded lists in the basal spelling series.

Ames reports that Betts made a careful survey in 1940 of seventeen basal

---

8. Ibid., p. 76–77.

spelling series. Betts found that each of these series included an average of 3,763 words, Grades 2-8. He also found that 543 of these words were in all seventeen of the series. What is even more significant, he found that there was unanimous grade placement agreement on only 1 word. In every series, *long* was placed at the second grade level. A similar study was conducted in 1949, with fewer spelling textbooks surveyed. This time Betts found slightly fewer total words (3,719), but more agreement concerning the words to be included: 483 words or 8 percent of the total as contrasted with 6 percent in the previous study. There was agreement concerning the grade placement of 65 words, with 55 of these words being placed at the second grade level. This still represents minimal consistency among various publishers.

Ames reports the results of his survey; he surveyed seven series, with a 1955–1960 copyright. The average number of words introduced was 3,209 (more than 500 words less than Bett's findings of 1940 and 1949), but the total for all seven series was 6,043, and there was agreement among the authors of the seven series on only 1,283 words.

To make even more pointed the grade placement discrepancy among the various series: one series places the word *teacher* at Grade 3; in another series *teachers* is placed at Grade 6. Another example: Series A considers *big* a Grade 2 word; *bigger* is a Grade 4 word in Series B, and Series C places *biggest* at Grade 5.[9]

In summarizing his own study, and contrasting it with the previous studies conducted by Emmett Betts, Ames writes:

> The evidence seems to indicate that there is still no great amount of agreement among authors of spelling textbooks with respect to spelling vocabulary that should be included in the elementary grades spelling program.
>
> Part of this lack of agreement may be explained by the fact that although all of the series are reportedly using the same research studies, different authors have emphasized certain studies more than others in citing research.
>
> Certainly all is not as it should be if one must wait three years before adding an "s" to the word teacher and treating this variant form as an entirely new word.[10]

In the past, and this tradition is still reflected in spelling series in use in our elementary schools, the 3,000 or 3,500 words included on most basic lists have been selected with reference to the following criteria:

1. How important or crucial is the word? (This criterion would eliminate certain scientific terms, even those words used in modern elementary science textbooks.)
2. How widespread is the use of the word? (Does a child who lives in Boston need to know how to spell *cactus;* does a child who lives in Phoenix need to know how to spell *harbor?*)
3. How frequently does the word appear on lists which result from careful studies of children's writing?

---

9. Wilbur Ames, "A Comparison of Spelling Textbooks," *Elementary English* 42 (1965): 146–52, 188.
10. Ibid., p. 188.

4. How difficult is the word to spell, and how serious (in terms of communication) is a spelling error likely to be?

Linguists would probably not ignore these criteria but would note that the emphasis has been, for too long, on the "communication" facet or objective of language, and that it is time more attention was paid to the structure of our language and the symbols which comprise relationships between spoken and written symbols. Squire writes:

> If one could pick one word to characterize our instructional programs in the English language arts during the past half century, I believe the key word would probably be communication. No other term, properly defined, so clearly indicates what we have been attempting in our classrooms; no other term so sharply indicates what we have selected, emphasized, rejected, and ignored.[11]

It is precisely this overriding concern for communication which has resulted in including on the same spelling list words which exemplify the usual influence of the "silent e" on the preceding vowel (*home, game, ride*), and words which are exceptions to the "rule," or variations of the pattern (*come, have, live*). It probably does not help children toward independence in spelling to organize lists in such an unsystematic manner.

The elementary teacher is presented with a dilemma which, to date, has not concerned the linguist. It is logical, orderly, and systematic to present words in groups which represent patterns: consonant-vowel-consonant (*had, bad, sad*); C-V-C + "silent e" (*save, gave, rave*); but it must surely be frustrating to a second-grade child whose spelling program is organized in this manner to attempt to write a letter, a story, a poem, or a simple report with only regularly patterned words at his command. It is difficult to organize much writing worthy of the term *creative* with such a limited vocabulary at the child's command. In short, the problem is this: which is to be preferred: a spelling program which presents words in an orderly sequence, patterned words selected because of the phoneme-grapheme correspondence they illustrate, or a spelling program which is based on selected samples of children's writing and which presents words researchers have found children need and use?

Sounds of English

Before discussing this issue any further, it would probably be wise to take a look at the sounds which combine to form our American English language and the relationship of these sounds to the phonological facets of letters used to represent them.

It has been suggested that spelling programs have been, and are, organized primarily with reference to written symbols, with only brief attention to the phonemes these graphemes represent.

---

11. James Squire, "New Directions in Language Learning," *Elementary English* 39 (1962): 535.

Hall, in his booklet *Sound and Spelling in English,* takes issue with the "writing" approach to spelling, the meaningless rote memorization of a series of letters. He asserts (as most structural linguists do) the primacy of speech over writing and writes:

> The consequence of this primacy of speech over writing is that we must not only analyze the situation but also formulate relationships and base our strategy (in this case, of course, teaching procedure) in terms of speech first and writing second. We cannot begin our analysis by taking up letters and the way they are "pronounced." We must first know what are the sounds of English and then must see how (and to what extent) they are represented in spelling. When we know the relationships of letters to sounds, we can then see whether there are degrees of complication in these relationships. In other words, whether some English spellings are more straightforward and systematic than others. If such degrees of complication exist in the way words are written we must classify them and take them into account when planning the order in which we teach our children to read and spell words.[12]

Hall's position on the basic issue which has been raised, structure or communication, is very clear. Whether it is a practical position for an elementary teacher faced with problems of motivation and the more or less immediate satisfaction of a child's need for a word is another issue. It is certainly of value to an elementary teacher to know something of the sounds which form the building blocks of our language.

Sounds are generally divided into two basic categories, *vowels* and *consonants.* There is a third category or group of sounds which do not fit neatly into either of the major categories, but the two major groups might be considered first.

Consonant Sounds. Consonant sounds are those produced when the breath stream is obstructed at any one of several points from lungs through windpipe and mouth. Consonant sounds are generally classified according to the characteristics of the obstruction; *where* the obstruction is formed in the mouth, *how* it is formed, and finally whether or not the vocal cords (*bands* or *folds* may be more accurate terms, but *vocal cords* is a term familiar to most readers) vibrate when the sound is made.

Where the sound is formed

labials: consonants formed with the lips
labio-dentals: consonants formed with the upper teeth and lower lip
dentals: consonants formed with the tip of the tongue against the inside of the upper front teeth
alveolars: consonants formed with the tip of the tongue against the gum ridge
palatals: consonants formed with the front of the tongue raised against the *front* of the palate
velars: consonants formed with the back of the tongue raised against the *back* of the palate

---

12. Robert Hall, *Sound and Spelling in English* (Philadelphia: Chilton Co., Book Division, 1961), p. 2.

Another way of classification is that of mode of articulation or the way in which the breath stream is obstructed:

How the sound is formed

fricatives: consonants formed by obstructing the breath stream so the breath streams evenly over the entire area of obstruction
sibilants: consonants formed with the breath stream partially obstructed but with the breath passing over the depression in the center of the tongue
affricates: consonants in which the breath stream is completely stopped then released slowly with a certain amount of friction
stops: consonants in which the air stream is completely stopped for a short time and then suddenly released
laterals: consonants formed with the breath forced over one or both sides of the tongue
retroflexes: consonants formed with the tip of the tongue curled or "turned" up in the back of the mouth
nasals: consonants produced with the nose used as a resonance chamber
voiced consonants: consonants formed with the vocal cords vibrating during production
voiceless consonants: consonants formed with the vocal cords quiet, *not* vibrating during production
aspirates: puffs of breath that occur during the release of the stop

It is perhaps worthy of reemphasis to note that in working with sounds, linguists may *represent* these sounds in isolation, for purposes of clarity, but sounds are never demonstrated in isolation. It is hardly possible to produce a consonant sound by itself. A consonant sound is almost invariably accompanied by at least the suggestion of a vowel sound; a "schwa" (short *u* or unaccented vowel sound) at the very least. It would not be particularly helpful to pronounce consonant sounds in isolation anyway, since the result is so artificial and so unlike the normal speech sounds the graphemes represent.

Knowledge of the phonemes of American English is important for the elementary teacher because it gives a solid and scientific basis to the work done in phonics. It should not have the unfortunate effect of causing the teacher to isolate these phonemes in work with children or to develop drill exercises in order that children may quickly identify and repeat them out of context and devoid of meaning.

Phonemes differ from language to language, and sounds which are significant in terms of differentiating meaning in one language are not significant in another. The difference in meaning between *sip* and *zip* in English causes us to classify the /s/ and /z/ as clearly different and separate phonemes. In Spanish, this difference is not crucial, so the sounds are not represented by different phonemes. The difference between *either* (\'ē-thər\) and *ether* (\'ē-thər\) has already been pointed out as an example of the need for different phonemic representations for the voiced and voiceless *th* sounds in American English.

Table 1 illustrates and categorizes the consonant sounds of American English. A phonemic transcription is given (that of the International Phonetic Alphabet), and the pronunciation key suggested in a widely used elementary school dictionary is also provided.[13]

TABLE 1

Phonemic Transcription and Dictionary Respelling
of the Consonant Phonemes of American English

The Initial Consonant of:	Technical Description	Phonemic Transcription	Dictionary Respelling
1. pin	voiceless bilabial stop	/p/	p
2. bin	voiced bilabial stop	/b/	b
3. tin	voiceless alveolar stop	/t/	t
4. din	voiced alveolar stop	/d/	d
5. kin	voiceless velar stop	/k/	k
6. get	voiced velar stop	/g/	g
7. fin	voiceless labial-dental fricative	/f/	f
8. vim	voiced labial-dental fricative	/v/	v
9. thin	voiceless inter-dental fricative	/θ/	th
10. this	voiced inter-dental fricative	/ð/	th
11. sin	voiceless dental sibilant	/s/	s
12. zip	voiced dental sibilant	/z/	z
13. shin	voiceless palatal sibilant	/š/ or /ʃ/	sh
14. azure	voiced palatal sibilant	/ž/ or /ʒ/	zh
15. chin	voiceless palatal affricate	/č/ or /tʃ/	ch
16. gin	voiced palatal affricate	/g/ or /dʒ/	j
17. mint	voiced labial nasal	/m/	m
18. name	voiced alveolar nasal	/n/	n
19. rim	voiced retroflex	/r/	r
20. limb	voiced alveolar lateral	/l/	l
21. hope	aspirate	/h/	h

If a consonant sound occurs in a medial position in a word, it is not quite the same as it is when the sound occurs at the beginning of a word. A lighted match would probably be extinguished by the /p/ at the beginning of *pie* or *pin*. This same match would remain lighted during the voicing of *clipper* or *lip,* at least as these words are normally pronounced. Such slight differences, differences which do *not* change meaning, are often termed *phonetic* differences by linguists. The terms *phoneme* and *phonemic* are usually reserved for significant units of speech sounds, units of sound which may be contrasted with similar sounds in order to express differences in meaning. The initial consonant sound in *pill,* the medial sound in

13. *Webster's New Elementary Dictionary* (Springfield, Mass.: G. & C. Merriam Co., 1970).

hoping, and the final sound in *hop* are not quite the same, although the same phonemic representation /p/ is used in each case. The differences do not cause problems in communication between one speaker of American English and another. If one used the slightly more plosive *p* generally used at the beginning of a word (*pipe*) in the middle or in the final position, meaning would not be affected. It is important in American English to differentiate between the /ʃ/ sound heard in wa*sh* and the /tʃ/ sound heard in wat*ch.* Therefore we need only one phonemic transcription for the several *p* sounds, but *two* symbols to contrast the final sounds in *cash* and *catch* (or wa*sh* and wat*ch*).

Vowel Sounds. Vowel sounds are those sounds which are produced without obstruction of the air stream. The stream of air from the lungs passes through the mouth without the obstruction associated with consonant sounds. It should be clearly understood that this discussion concerns vowel *sounds,* not the vowel letters. There are only seven letters, sometimes combined, sometimes used singly, to represent a minimum of eleven vowel sounds (not including digraphs and diphthongs).[14]

Vowel sounds are classified rather simply by the position of the tongue in the mouth as the vowel sound is produced. The height of the tongue classifies a vowel as high (*like, look, feet, fit*), middle (*bought, cut*), or low (*hot, cat*). Front (*cat, let*), central (*cut, hot*), and back (*look, coat*) are further descriptions of the tongue's position when the vowel is formed. *Lax* and *tense* are the terms used to describe the tension of the tongue as the vowel is formed. The tongue is somewhat

TABLE 2

Phonemic Transcription and Dictionary Respellings of the Vowel Phonemes of American English

The Vowel Sound of:	Phonemic Description	IPA Kenyon-Pike	Trager-Smith	Dictionary Respelling*
1. boot	high-back-tense	/u/	/uw/†	ü
2. look	high-back-lax	/ū/	/u/	u̇
3. coat	mid-back-tense	/o/	/ow/	ō
4. bought	mid-back-lax	/ɔ/	/o/	ô
5. cut	mid-central-lax	/ə/	/ə/	u
6. hot	low-central-lax	/a/	/a/	o
7. cat	low-front-lax	/æ/	/æ/	a
8. let	mid-front-lax	/ɛ/	/e/	e
9. wait	mid-front-tense	/e/	/ey/	ā
10. fit	high-front-lax	/ɪ/	/i/	i
11. feet	high-front-tense	/i/	/iy/	ē

  * *Thorndike-Barnhart Beginning Dictionary,* 8th ed. (Chicago: Scott Foresman & Co., 1974).

  † This is actually a sequence of two phonemes, according to Trager and Smith.

14. Consult the Glossary for definitions of these terms.

relaxed in forming the vowel sound heard in *look*. It is more tense in forming the vowel sound heard in *seat*.

Y /y/ and *w* /w/ may be considered *semivowels* or *glides*. They are similar to vowels in the way they are produced, but, like consonants, they always occur with a vowel as the nucleus of a syllable. The term *glide* refers to a movement—up and forward for the *y* (*yard*), up and backward for the *w* (*warm*).

When a vowel phoneme is followed by a semivowel, the resulting sound is called a *diphthong*. Table 3 represents some of the more significant diphthongs of American English.

TABLE 3

Phonemic Transcription and Dictionary Respelling
of the Diphthongs of American English

The Diphthong of:	IPA Kenyon-Pike	Trager-Smith*	Dictionary Respelling†
1. light, white, etc.	/ay/	/ay/	ī
2. how, crowd, etc.	/aw/	/aw/	ou
3. toy, oil, etc.	/ɔy/	/oy/	oi

*See note about phonemes from table 2.

†*Thorndike-Barnhart Beginning Dictionary,* 8th ed. (Chicago: Scott Foresman & Co., 1974).

Perhaps two points are worth restating:

1. Linguists do not agree on the number of phonemes in our language. Although specific numbers—thiry-eight, forty, forty-four, forty-seven—may be stated by certain writers, the reader should understand that dialectal variations and differences in the operational definition of *significant* can and do cause the number of phonemes quoted to vary. The important concept for an elementary teacher to grasp is probably an understanding of a "phonetic" difference as contrasted with a "phonemic" difference. A *phonemic* difference affects meaning (*zip, sip*); a *phonetic* difference typically does not (in *pepper* the /p/ sounds somewhat different in the two positions; the difference does not affect meaning).

2. Most linguists agree that vowel and consonant sounds should not be studied in isolation. Any given vowel or consonant sound exists in a relationship to other sounds in a word. Indeed, a good case could be made for not studying sounds in isolated words. A phoneme will be pronounced differently if the word in which it occurs occupies a stressed position in an utterance rather than an unstressed position. The primary teacher, especially, may smile indulgently at the suggestion that he work on initial consonants as they exist in paragraphs and sentences. Nonetheless, it is not too much to ask this teacher not to commit the error of asking children to repeat in chorus "t-tuh, tuh, tuh, v-vuh, vuh, vuh . . . and so forth." Sounds do vary according to their position within a word, and a sound repeated in isolation is of little value in learning

phoneme-grapheme correspondence for purposes of spelling or reading. Sounds have been listed in isolation for purposes of identification by teachers and to help the readers understand the linguists' efforts at identification of the significant sound units of American English.

Dictionary Respelling and the Role of the Dictionary in Spelling Programs in Elementary Schools

Two widely used systems of dictionary respellings were included in the preceding section of this chapter. Most elementary teachers agree that instruction in the use of the dictionary is assuming a more important role than ever before in reading and spelling programs. Several trends seem to be developing:

1. The use of the dictionary is encouraged at the primary level. Traditionally the dictionary has been introduced perhaps only to the extent of learning the function of guide words and entry words at the fourth grade level. At least one publisher begins dictionary work in the first grade and assumes a significant amount of understanding of the organization and function of the dictionary by the third grade.

2. Lexicographers are encouraging the understanding of the differences between spoken language and the written representation of speech. This is clearly evident in dictionary entries which show syllable divisions. For example:

au·thor·i·ty   \ə-'thȯr-ət-ē\ [15]

    In writing *authority,* if there is a need to divide the word, the first entry tells one how this is usually done—the accepted form. The second entry, a respelling, tells the reader how most educated speakers of American English pronounce the word.

3. Pupils are (or should be) encouraged to check more than one source for definitions and respellings, including the symbols used for sounds and indication of accent or stress. A widely used dictionary respells *authority* as follows:

au thor ity   (ə thôr′ ə tē) [16]

Compare this with the first respelling above.

    Differences in the respelling of other words are even more apparent:

	Thorndike-Barnhart	Webster's
aware	(ə wər′ or ə war′)	\ə-'waər\
cupboard	(kub′ ərd)	\'kəb-ərd\
draw	(dro)	\'drȯ\
entertainment	(en′ tər tān′ mənt)	\ˌent-ər-'tān-mənt\

---

15. *Webster's New Elementary Dictionary,* p. 34.
16. *Thorndike-Barnhart Beginning Dictionary,* 8th ed.

This list could be extended indefinitely. There are differences in the representation of vowel sounds, in the indication of syllable accents or stresses, and even in syllable divisions (note *entertainment*).

After reviewing five dictionaries, each developed by reputable lexicographers and each widely used, Emery cites a thirty-nine-word sentence which could be written in 11,997,440 ways. Emery notes: "The possibility of teacher-student conflict over what words are to be called misspelled is ever present unless the teacher arbitrarily establishes one dictionary as the sole authority, an unhappy and impractical solution which might suggest to some students that other dictionaries simply duplicate entries or are unreliable."[17]

Nowhere is disagreement or difference of opinion among linguists more obvious than in an area like this one! One dictionary respelling is not more "scientific," more "linguistically sound" than another. The linguist whose research indicates that the first syllable of *entertainment* ends with the first *t* is not more correct than the linguist who says it ends with the first *n;* the two are merely operating on the basis of different data.

Children can learn a great deal by exposure to, and study of, at least these two major dictionaries which are so widely used in elementary schools. There is some controversy regarding this position, but it would seem that the values of using more than one dictionary would outweigh the dangers of confusing children in the early stages of learning the use and function of this important tool. Granting the possibility of such confusion in the initial phases of learning about the dictionary, there nevertheless seems to be little reason for not providing a number of dictionaries representing different linguistic points of view and different difficulty levels for fifth and sixth graders. There are more commercially published picture dictionaries than ever before, and of course, primary teachers can provide the time, the materials, and the guidance for children to construct their own dictionaries or word books.

4. Dictionaries can help children to understand that several pronunciations of a particular word are acceptable. The child who says \en-'dùr\ is not more correct than the child who says \en-'dyùr\. The child whose *r* at the end of *car* is no more definite or even less pronounced than the *r* at the end of *draw* is not or should not be considered funny or peculiar. Pronunciation differences were responsible for the creation of Noah Webster's famous *Blue-Back Speller*. Webster considered standardization of American English essential for a developing nation—dialectal differences were symptomatic of other divisions and were unhealthy in a group of jealous and loosely confederated states only lately joined together. Surely we are more tolerant of such differences today —even as radio and television and population mobility work toward acquainting us with the many dialects which give richness to American English.

The social stigma attached to poor spelling has already been mentioned. Adults and children alike receive the advice to "check the dictionary" when unsure of a spelling. It has also been noted that a word's pronunciation may not be a very reliable guide to its spelling. Does *phase* begin with *ph* or *f*? Is the second con-

---

17. Donald Emery, *Variant Spellings in Modern American Dictionaries* (Champaign, Ill.: National Council of Teachers of English, 1973), p. 2.

sonant sound represented by an *s* or *z*? It is unfortunately true that one must know a little of how a word is spelled before a dictionary is very much help.

A dictionary is of considerable assistance in pronouncing a word according to "standard" practice when one encounters an unfamiliar word in reading. A dictionary is a guide to standard practice—what is accepted, at this moment in time, by educated people in terms of spelling, pronunciation, and definition. It is not and should not be considered a "rule book," a standard setter, or an arbiter of "the best" in our language. It is a photograph, or a mirror, of our language, not a linguistic Roberts's *Rules of Order*.

Variation among the standard and carefully prepared dictionaries is not frowned upon by most linguists. It is one of the marks of a growing, living language, which English certainly is, that dictionaries must be revised in terms of current accepted practice and scientific analysis of the language and that lexicographers and phoneticians will have some scholarly disagreements regarding the direction of the growth and extent of linguistic change.

What can the dictionary—or several different dictionaries—contribute to the spelling program? The most obvious contribution is to the breadth and depth of meanings of a word a child is learning to spell. *Webster's New Elementary Dictionary* (designed for use in third and fourth grades) lists three different meanings or definitions for the word *cool*. *Dock* is provided five different entries, and one entry for *dock* includes three related but somewhat different definitions. However, it is recognized that there are many who regard a dictionary in a manner somewhat more sacred than that which has been suggested here.

If a linguistically oriented spelling program, organized on the basis of common patterns—*pan, man, fan; gave, save, rave,* and so forth—is used, the elementary teacher must make certain that the process of deriving spelling generalizations from exposure to a series of patterns is not completely devoid of meaning. While the common patterns of our language do form a reasonable structure upon which a spelling program can be built, very few elementary teachers would be satisfied with spelling lists which are meaningless combinations of letters, alike except for an initial consonant or a final silent *e*. The dictionary can be a tremendous aid in supplying a basic definition for a completely unfamiliar word, and for adding to the meanings a child can supply for words he may know a little about—words which may be in his speaking vocabulary but not in his writing vocabulary.

The dictionary can help children pronounce words as they are usually pronounced and to accept more than one pronunciation as "standard." Finally, although elementary school children should seldom be asked to write dictionary respellings, such respellings do help a child to see that the same sound may be represented in writing in a number of different ways. For example:

The sound of:

ā or /e/	ē or /iy/	i or /ay/
as it occurs in:		
bay, say	be, me, he	fly, by, my
weigh	free, see	white, bite
convey	receive	flight, bright
late, bake	believe	guy, buy
wait	dream, cream	trial, file

Because the vowel sounds in each of the columns are similar enough to be represented by the same phonemic symbols, the initial work in exercises of this type should probably be oral. After some work on the chalkboard or worksheets prepared by the teacher, children could refer to their dictionaries to see what different spelling patterns could be added to the lists and what additional examples could be found for the different spellings already indicated.

Spelling Patterns and Spelling Programs

The authors of *Spelling: Structure and Strategies* write:

> Spelling ability is a *learned* behavior. Ideally, what is learned is the structure of the writing system and how this system, with its alphabetic base, reflects the spoken language. This learning is accomplished through the multisensory-multimotor mechanisms that are involved in the act of spelling—audition, speech, vision and haptics—and the utilization of the resulting sensory impressions in developing a cognitive map of the orthography.[18]

While a program based upon the sequence of patterns suggested in this section cannot accomplish all of the goals or objectives suggested in the above statement, it is proposed that such a sequence will aid the pupil in acquiring some essential understandings of phoneme-grapheme correspondences.

This, essentially, is the linguists' plea: present spelling lists in an organized manner which will help children quite easily and with little effort to spell not only those words on the list, but words with similar patterns. The utility of these patterns for a given child's writing or the writing of a group of children is another issue, and this will be discussed further. Some attention should be given to these patterns. At the outset the reader should be warned that linguists disagree about the comprehensiveness and adequacy of these patterns just as they disagree about the number of phonemes of our American English language.

Pattern One

This is the most common pattern, and it consists of a consonant, a vowel, and a consonant (C-V-C). In Pattern One, the vowel is always a short vowel. The following words are examples of Pattern One words, with blends (consonant clusters) substituted for the initial or final consonants in some cases:

cat	bad	dig	drip	dent	hand
hat	sad	fig	trip	sent	band
sat	had	wig	strip	rent	sand
bat	mad	pig			
fat	dad	rig			

---

18. Hanna, Hodges, and Hanna, *Spelling: Structure and Strategies*, p. 109.

In helping children to understand Pattern One, and to decode words which fit this pattern, the following exercises might be used:

a. Change the initial consonants:

*b*ad→	*s*ad→	*h*ad→	*gl*ad
*b*ed→	*r*ed→	*sl*ed→	*bl*ed
*r*an→	*f*an→	*pl*an→	*cl*an

(Initial consonant clusters and digraphs may also be introduced. Consistency with the phonetic skills sequence of the reading program used should be considered here.)

b. Change the final consonants:

pa*n*→	pa*d*→	pa*t*
ba*n*→	ba*nd*→	ba*nk*

(Again, clusters may be used as the children develop skills in auditory discrimination.)

c. Substitute for the given vowel:

p*a*t   p*e*t   p*i*t   p*o*t

("Short" vowels only, at first, because they are more common and consistent in the way they are pronounced.)

Pattern Two

This pattern consists of a consonant, a vowel, a second consonant, and a final *e* (C-V-C + *e*). Examples and exceptions should probably be discussed separately, not in the same lesson. For instance, in one spelling book, designed for use at Grade Two, the following list appears: *car, come, came, kitten, like, likes, take,* and *make.* Five of these eight words follow Pattern Two. However, if children are to learn this generalization, then *come* and *make* do *not* belong in the same list. The major generalization to be drawn from exposure to these two words on the same list is that American English spelling is indeed so erratic as to make generalizing impossible and tedious memorization the only alternative.

There are a number of common words which follow Pattern Two, resulting in a "long" sound for the first vowel. This pattern typically refers to words in which the silent *e* "cues" the reader-speller to a long vowel sound:

save	hive	drove
gave	drive	tone
game	like	home
came	bike	

Suggested exercises for demonstrating the utility of this pattern might be as follows:

a. What happens to these words when a final *e* is added:

pan	plan	glad	can
pane	plane	glade	cane

b. What word follows the pattern:

pin	fin	win	tin	mad	bad	pan	man
p*i*ne	f*i*ne	w*i*ne	t*i*ne	_____	ba*d*e	_____	ma*n*e

c. Fill in the blanks: (Check the italicized word first!)

1. *Can* you cut the sugar _____?
2. I *plan* to fly the _____.
3. The *pin* was found beneath the _____ tree.

Teachers are well aware of how frequently words occur that are exceptions to Pattern Two—*love, have, give, come.* These exceptions are significant not only because they are numerous, but because they are so commonly used! That is, the exceptions form a major part of the child's reading and spelling vocabularies. One estimate states that the "silent *e*" rule is valid for only about two-thirds of our American English words.[19] Should such a pattern be taught? Is a "half-generalization" worth learning? Perhaps it is! Knowledge of a pattern which children can use to unlock or decode half to two-thirds of the words they need to write is better than guesswork—50 percent to 66 percent better, in fact.

How does the teacher help the child handle the exceptions? After the generalization is operational for most of the children, the exceptions, their frequency and significance, can be discussed. Children will probably enjoy finding exceptions to this "rule" just as they were interested in studying words and in developing the original generalization.

Pattern Three

This pattern consists of a consonant, two vowels (which produce a diphthong or long vowel sound), and a consonant (C-V-V-C). Examples of words within this pattern:

rain	leaf	coat	need
grain	feast	goat	seed
train	least	float	feed
			greed

Elementary teachers will recognize this immediately as the old "When two vowels go walking, the first one does the talking," a mnemonic device in a more sophisticated dress. The results of Clymer's study are especially devastating to this rule. His findings suggest that it is useful in less than half of the words primary level children encounter when reading. The exceptions are well known—*relief, brief, break, bear,* and so forth. Presumably this problem could be handled as were the exceptions in Pattern Two—generalization first, then exceptions.

---

19. Theodore Clymer, "The Utility of Phonic Generalizations in the Primary Grades," *The Reading Teacher* 16 (1963): 252–58.

The following exercises may be helpful in developing this generalization:

a. What word:

    begins like *fun*, ends like *need*? _____

    begins like *trip*, ends like *rain*? _____

    begins like *boy*, ends like *coat*? _____

b. Add to these lists:

seed	lean	fail
need	meat	trail
____	____	____

c. Finish the second line:

    The first vowel sound in *lean* is like the vowel sound in *he*.

    The first vowel sound in *break* is like the vowel sound in _____

    (*cake, paint*).

These patterns account for the vast majority of American English spellings. There are others which are perhaps significant enough to mention, at least briefly.

Pattern Four

This is a consonant-vowel (C-V) pattern. Examples are:

be	go	by
me	so	my
he	no	try

Words which include two vowel *letters* but only one vowel *sound* are also included in this pattern; for example: *day, play, say; flee, bee, see; die, lie;* and so forth.[20] There is a good bit of stability to this pattern except when the vowel is an *o*. The reader will immediately think of *to, do,* and *too* as exceptions to the pattern generalization.

Excercises which may help in developing this generalization:

a. Add to the lists, using the same vowel sounds:

we	sky
knee	why
____	____
____	____

b. Make rhyming sentences with the following words:

    by and try

    we and he

c. What word do you "make" when you add the letter *k* at the beginning and letter *w* to the end of *no*? Use the word in a sentence.

---

20. It is recognized that diphthongs are represented by the letters *au* and *ie*.

Change letters for the first sound in *so* to the letters for first sound in *snip*. Now, add a letter *w* to the *o*. What word do you have now? Use the word in a sentence.

Pattern Five

The *r* controlled vowel presents many problems in English. Usually, the vowel preceding an *r* is neither long nor short. For example:

far	bird	clear	bore
farm	word	fear	born
charm	heard	cheer	form
car	burn	dear, deer	sort

The variety of spelling patterns possible here is apparent. It may well be misleading to consider this a pattern at all, since it includes so much. It is also true that dialectal variations will cause differences in the pronunciation of these words. Words like *or* and *for* are pronounced quite differently when they occupy positions of strong stress and weak stress in sentences. The reader might read the following sentences (aloud) as naturally as possible.

1. (Firmly) Will you do it *or* shall I?
   (Easily) Are *you* driving or is *Dick?*
2. that this nation *of* the people, *by* the people, and *for* the people . . .
3. Sit *still! I'll* get the book for you.
   Sit still! I'll get the book *for* you.

Could you hear the difference that stress makes? The exercise above, incidentally, can be varied, extended, and/or simplified to make the same point with children.

What can be done about the variety of spellings for the consonant, plus the vowel influenced by r, plus the consonant pattern—*heard, burn, third?* We have probably reached the place where patterning isn't much help. Children may have to give special attention to such spellings as these—however, not as "demons" or "trouble-spot" words.[21] It has been fairly well established that pointing out trouble-spots, especially if this is done prior to giving a child a chance to learn the word, is of little value. Trouble may be created rather than avoided! Perhaps one of the following approaches could be used:

Grade One or early Grade Two:

a. Listen to these words: *stern, burn, learn.* What do you notice? Now look at them on this chart/chalkboard. What letters do you see to represent the vowel sound in these words?

Grade Two or Grade Three:

a. Word, third, and *curd* all sound something alike. Can anyone tell us how one of these words is spelled? Another? What other words have this "vowel + *r*"

---

21. The results of Project 1991 might be recalled here; about 3 percent of the words "fed" to the computer could not be correctly spelled, using generalizations appropriate to American English. There really aren't *that* many demons.

sound? (Perhaps the children are familiar with the term *schwa;* if so, this could be used.) Let's list some on the board.

b. What *r* or "vowel + *r*" sounds are spelled as they are in the word *heard?* The word *turn?* The word *stern* (as in the stern of a boat)? Let's put these at the top of three different columns and see what other words we can add to these lists.

Grade Three or Grade Four:

a. Children might use their dictionaries to add to a list such as the one started above. Given the types of experiences suggested above, children may be skillful enough so that this could be an independent activity or seatwork.

How Much Emphasis on Patterns?

There is perhaps no more controversial area than this one, among linguists and between linguists and educators. One answer to this problem is to use the best of both approaches. In the primary grades, it should not take an abnormal amount of time to do some work with the three most basic patterns. Worksheets, dittoed or mimeographed, could be developed and could supplement the basal spelling book, if it is organized according to need or interest or based on a study of children's writing.

Conversely, if the basic spelling work is with patterns, then the teacher has a responsibility not to neglect the communication aspect of spelling. It would be unfortunate if children had few writing experiences aside from practicing patterns in list forms or filling in the blanks. It may be true that communication has been overstressed to the detriment of developing an understanding of the structure of our language. However, we shouldn't lose sight of the communication function in a headlong rush to correct past mistakes. The proof of the success of *any* approach to teaching spelling is in children's ability to spell correctly and in their desire to do this for purposes of clear and unimpeded writing communication. The first part of this objective may be achieved through children's maintenance of functional individual lists, their study of the major spelling patterns of our language, or the use of a standard "Most Frequently Used" word list. These approaches are not mutually exclusive at all. Earlier in the chapter, a great deal of time and space was devoted to a discussion of the contradictory research in this area. Until the research guidelines for spelling programs point more clearly in the direction of almost complete reliance upon a study of patterns, it seems a little unwise to ignore these other approaches.

Linguists have made strong and earnest pleas for a holistic, unsegmented study of language in elementary classrooms—reading should be related to speech; writing should be related to speech and reading; grammar should be based on oral language, and so forth. The study of patterns in isolation, without concern for use or function, is apt to distort words which might better be viewed in a more utilitarian manner. It is not unrealistic to expect an elementary teacher to use appropriate elements from both areas.

Materials for Teaching Spelling

Dictionaries are of obvious benefit to a spelling program, for reasons already mentioned. Many copies of many dictionaries at several levels of difficulty, from picture dictionaries through junior and even college dictionaries, will be useful, from third grade on. Special dictionaries or glossaries, prepared by the children, to accompany a science or social studies project or unit will help children's spelling as well as add interest to the content field.

To reinforce the point made about acceptance of dialectal differences, the tape recorder is quite useful. Almost every aspect of auditory discrimination can be strengthened by the use of appropriate and rather inexpensive teacher-made tapes. The first tapes might be designed to sensitize children's concepts of gross discrimination—wind, running water. Other tapes could present series of words alike except for initial or final consonants (voices other than the classroom teacher's might hold children's attention longer). Children themselves might help in preparing tapes(assuming there is no serious articulatory problem).

All that has been said about the presentation of patterns is not meant to preclude children's keeping individual word lists. Some teachers find that word boxes work best, with unfamiliar words entered on three-by-five-inch cards. These could be organized by topic, alphabetically, and/or by patterns. Shorthand notebooks can serve the same general purpose as the boxes and are easier to carry to a carrel or home for some needed review.

The spelling text is probably not enough by itself. A textbook advertisement claims:

a modern, practical word list arranged in linguistic patterns and based on frequency of use as indicated by children's literature and textbooks; . . . *extra overprinted teachers' editions showing how to elicit correct response to sound so that the teacher needs no special training in linguistics.*

Even these rather fulsome claims tacitly acknowledge the influence of the teacher with its "help" which supersedes the need for special linguistic training on the part of the teacher. Most authors of most series freely admit that the most carefully, "scientifically," selected word lists do not constitute a completely adequate spelling program. A basal series in spelling does offer a sequential, organized program. It also saves a teacher the time and effort required to prepare skill sheets and other practice material. The teacher is, as usual, responsible for supplying whatever is missing. If the text emphasizes patterns, more functional writing is needed as a supplement. If functional lists are basic to the text, then the supplement would be in the nature of some pattern work. A balanced spelling program probably includes both. This seems to be the best approach, until research on the utility of patterns as a total approach to studying and learning the principles governing spelling in American English provides more definitive evidence. Incomplete as spelling programs have been, and are, we lack sufficient evidence that the linguists, with their sophisticated phonetic approach, offer genuine improvement. In an article in *Elementary*

English, Yee states what seems to be a most sensible position, for the time being at least:

> The burden of proof for pedagogical applications, therefore, rests on the shoulders of advocates for increased emphasis on phonetic approaches. Yet the classroom results may still be similar to earlier studies on the question of instruction in spelling rules, for the preponderance of studies appear to question the effectiveness of strict phonetic approaches. The degree of benefits and the extent of limitations obtained through predominant reliance on spelling generalizations in spelling programs have yet to be established by empirical research on such application. Significant results supporting the use of a few rules provides little proof that a major emphasis on rules in spelling would be successful.[22]

Dr. Yee concludes his article by stating:

> In the controversy between spelling rules or no spelling rules, the false dichotomy should be apparent. A review of the more carefully written works on the issue shows that the question of spelling generalization may be maturing into one of degree and points to the need to fully investigate classroom applications before curriculum materials and methods are recommended for classroom use.[23]

Evaluation of Spelling Programs

Assessment of the success of a program, or of a child's progress in a program, is closely related to the objectives of that program. It is hardly fair, or even sensible, to measure what one did not attempt to teach, or to gauge a child's progress toward a goal one did not recognize as worth reaching. Thus, the linguists say very little about attitudes toward correct spelling, or the acquisition of a functional spelling vocabulary. Rudorf lists what many linguists would agree is a relatively complete list of objectives or goals for the spelling program in an elementary school. He writes:

> The abilities we would then be trying to develop would include:
> 1. the ability to discriminate between the phonemes of a language.
> 2. the ability to identify the graphemic options of each of the phonemes.
> 3. the ability to identify syllables in oral speech.
> 4. the ability to recognize stress when present.
> 5. the ability to relate phonemes to their immediate environment.
> 6. the ability to recognize morphemes (meaningful units of phoneme combinations) such as roots, affixes, and inflections.
> 7. the ability to utilize certain principles of morphonemics (how morphemes change in combination to form words; for example, the process of assimilation and synthesis).

---

22. Albert Yee, "The Generalization Controversy in Spelling Instruction," *Elementary English* 43 (1966): 159–60.
23. Ibid., p. 161.

8. the ability to relate meaning (as determined by syntax) to spelling (the homonym problem).[24]

One can test or measure the achievement of objectives such as these. Children can be exposed to words which are unknown, even nonsense syllables, to see which principles or generalizations children can apply. (Nonsense syllables are not as useless as they might seem; the request to write "sig," "teg," and "bap" would test children's operational understanding of Pattern One, C-V-C.) This is *not* to recommend the frequent use of nonsense syllables, only to suggest that their incorporation in a spelling testing program might provide some useful data for a teacher—and the pupil as well.

Because generalizations are taught and learned for purposes of transfer, it would not be especially profitable to test for the ability to spell only those words previously studied. A major portion of the words in a testing program should be words to which children have had little previous exposure; otherwise, it is memorization and recall which is being tested, not the application of a generalization. The child may be asked to write examples of words which fit a pattern and which he has not studied; he might also be asked to write as *many* words which sound like and are spelled like a given word as he can.

Because even those students of the phonology of our language who claim a highly significant degree of phoneme-grapheme correspondence admit there are some words which simply don't pattern, the testing program will probably include some words which the child has looked at, memorized, and is now asked to repeat correctly, it is to be hoped. Linguists say little about this, but it is assumed that they would favor the frequent checking of children's written work. This tells the teacher, and the pupil, whether or not a pattern generalization, or a memorized nonpattern word, is operational and functional for a child. It does seem that it is important to know whether a child can spell in lifelike situations requiring correct spelling—letters, reports, stories, essays. In a similar vein, although Rudorf's list included no reference to the development of positive attitudes toward spelling, most elementary teachers work toward developing such attitudes. It may be true that a thorough understanding of the three, or four, or eight basic patterns of American English is all a child needs in order to acquire an interest in correct spelling and a willingness to proofread before submitting or mailing. There is probably more to be done than drilling on patterns, however. Children probably need to be given time to proofread, and folders of written work need to be kept in order to reassure them (and their teachers) that some progress has been made. Comments on spelling may be a part of a pupil-teacher writing conference, and the teacher may keep notes regarding the types of problems a child is having.

Techniques which a teacher has typically found useful in evaluating a child's progress and growth in spelling are not inappropriate if the nature of the words selected for study change. The linguist's recommendations apply primarily to stressing patterns and generalizations about sound-letter relationships; less em-

---

24. E. Hugh Rudorf., Jr., "Measurement of Spelling Ability," *Elementary English* 42 (1965): 893.

phasis is placed upon the lexical function of a word in a phrase, a sentence, or a paragraph. Teachers may consider their evaluation procedures somewhat inadequate if they do not include an assessment of the child's ability to use a word, correctly, in a report, a theme, or a story. It is probably correct to say that the measurement procedures used by an elementary teacher who includes in his spelling program the application of some linguistic principles will extend somewhat beyond those aspects that concern the linguist.

Summary

English is not an easy language to learn to spell; one reason is that there are only twenty-six letters in the alphabet to symbolize from thirty-five to forty-five or forty-seven significant sound units. There have been several different proposals for solving this problem. Special alphabets, augmentation of the traditional alphabet, like i/t/a, have found support. Simplified spelling has also been proposed. Most simplified spelling programs utilize the traditional alphabet, but reduce the number of options for spelling words—*leave* might be spelled *leev; seem* would retain its traditional spelling; and *relief* could be consistently spelled *releef.*

How serious is the discrepancy between the grapheme and the phoneme in American English? This is an area of some controversy. One respected student of language, Clarence Barnhart, claims that the alphabet "misleads us" about 85 percent of the time. The results of recent studies at Stanford University, conducted under the direction of Dr. Paul Hanna, indicate that the sound-letter correspondence is much higher—up to 80 or 90 percent of our words are spelled consistently following a few basic patterns with some variations.

Whatever the extent of this lack of correspondence, there is obviously enough grapheme-phoneme inconsistency to cause some problems for children learning to read and spell our language. There appear to be several reasons for this inconsistency. First of all, speech came long before writing, and any writing system is a rather poor symbolization of human speech. English-speaking people have a linguistic heritage of Anglo-Saxon and of borrowing from Latin and Greek. In addition to this, words have been borrowed from other modern languages—French, Spanish, German, Italian. It is probably too much to expect entirely consistent spelling patterns in a language which has such a rich, but varied, history.

When the printing press assumed an influential position in communicating ideas, consistent spelling was dealt another blow. Prior to the invention of movable type, people wrote very much as they talked. Since one usually wrote to people whose dialects were similar to his, spelling was not particularly a problem. The audience for printed material was somewhat larger, however, and those who were employed to operate the presses often practiced "creative" spelling. Printers were not always well educated, and undoubtedly some of our more inconsistent and confusing spelling patterns can be traced to mistakes made by early printers which soon became entrenched in our language. The earliest dictionaries served to standardize further some printers' errors.

Attitudes of the general public toward correct spelling have changed. No longer are people casual about written communications. Correct spelling, in letters, notes, even memoranda, is assumed and expected. Helping pupils assume responsibility for correct spelling is one of a teacher's most challenging tasks.

Several phonemic transcriptions and phonetic alphabets suggest the marked contrast between the letters of our alphabet and the sounds these letters represent. There are approximately eleven sounds represented by five vowel letters in American English, and about twenty-two consonant sounds are represented by twenty-one consonant letters. In addition to these, linguists have identified two semivowels and three diphthongs. These two principles regarding sounds have been stressed a number of times in this chapter:

1. The term *phoneme* refers to the significant speech sounds of a language. These significant sounds are not the same in all languages, and some languages have a much closer letter-sound correspondence than English has.
2. Although linguists and lexicographers must be able to represent isolated sounds, this is, at its base, artificial. Sounds vary according to their position in a word (stressed and unstressed syllables) and the position of a word in a sentence (strong to weak stress). Drill on consonant and vowel sounds isolated from a word (some would say from a phrase in a sentence) serves little purpose in elementary school spelling and reading programs.

Dictionary respellings of words can serve to help children pronounce words as most educated people do and can help them see the variety of spellings a particular sound may have in English. In addition to providing help with pronunciation, the dictionary serves many other purposes in a modern spelling program. It can help children broaden and add depth to their vocabularies and is a useful check on the correct spelling of an unfamiliar word. However, it would be a serious error for teachers or children to think of a dictionary as a "standard setter" or rule book of our language. A dictionary reflects what *is;* it does not tell us what *should* be. The use of several dictionaries is recommended, in spite of the possibility of some confusion. The use of several dictionaries can do a great deal to help children grasp the arbitrary nature of our language and the diversity and riches which are such important characteristics of American English. It is possible to give so much emphasis to "Give a (or worse, *the*) definition of . . . ," or "Find *the* dictionary respelling for . . ." that an important linguistic generalization may escape children.

The utility of the dictionary as a basic tool in spelling programs is seldom questioned. There is much more controversy regarding the role of the spelling text. Very few educators advocate complete reliance upon a single textbook which comes to be regarded as *the* spelling program. A point which should not be overlooked in discussing the role of the spelling textbooks is the lack of consistency among the various texts. Although the majority of spelling programs claim to be based on the results of studies of children's writing, and the grade placement of words is based on surveys of the vocabularies basic to social studies, science, and reading programs, the same word will very seldom be placed at the same grade level in two or more spelling series. If vocabulary studies pointed in a stable and consistent direction for spelling lists—by series or by grade placement—we might be able to place more reliance on spelling textbooks. If one could assume that children in inner-city, suburban, and rural consolidated schools needed or frequently used nearly identical lists in their writing, the spelling text would be a more dependable guide to proficiency in spelling. As it is, most teachers supplement the textbook with group lists (agreed upon by a committee or the entire class as significant and worth learning for a specific purpose) and individual lists (comprising those words which are primarily significant to one child because he uses them in his personal and practical writing).

Linguists advocate basing the "core" of the spelling progam on the expansion of several spelling patterns. The simplest of these is the C-V-C pattern (*had, tan, big*). Another is the C-V-C silent *e* pattern. In Pattern Two words, the reader-speller is cued to a long vowel sound by the presence of the silent *e* (*hive, gave, home*). There are many many exceptions to this pattern, and many of the exceptions are very common words (*have, give, come*). In general, it is recommended that the "regular" pattern be introduced and then the exceptions. In words which conform to Pattern Three (C-V-V-C), the two vowel letters represent one vowel sound and this is the long sound. The reader is reminded that there are a great many exceptions to this pattern, too. How many exceptions and how significant these exceptions are is a matter of some controversy, but nonetheless this pattern should not be taught or learned as foolproof or "never-fail." Another pattern which has some significance is the C-V pattern (*he, we, my*), and some linguists recommend stressing the spelling pattern(s) which indicate the influence of an *r* on the preceding vowel (*heard, car, sort*). This is a particularly complex and difficult pattern because the pronunciation of the vowel, and the *r* as well, varies according to the regional dialects spoken and the position of the word in the phrase, sentence, and paragraph.

The authors and publishers of spelling texts are no less aware of developments in the field of linguistics than are the publishers of reading texts, and an increasing number of spelling texts will utilize the data regarding phoneme-grapheme correspondences in organizing and presenting spelling lists. If the spelling program is basically a process of generalizing from these patterns, then the nature of the supplemental lists would become more functional, and so would the guidance provided by the teacher. If the spelling text presents words on the basis of studies of children's writing and frequency counts of missed words, then the teacher can provide some valuable assistance by developing the pattern generalizations with children.

When words like *home* and *come* are presented in the same spelling lesson, children are forced to conclude that memorizing words, letter by letter, is the only way to succeed in spelling. Learning how to expand patterns, on the other hand, promotes independence and greater self-reliance in decoding unfamiliar words.

Until further research gives us more detailed information about the extent of phoneme-grapheme correspondence in American English, it is probably not very wise to place complete dependence upon the pattern approach to spelling. Some emphasis upon patterns would seem to promote more independence and more confidence with unfamiliar words. Pattern work needs to be supplemented by individual help with words that children actually need for their writing. A first grader who feels comfortable with Patterns One and Two still has a somewhat limited writing vocabulary. It may be assumed that linguists would not favor limiting children's writing until all basic patterns had been introduced. Some linguists have charged that communication has far too long served as the only goal of language arts programs, to the detriment of knowledge of structure. The balance between these two goals, obviously both desirable and worth achieving, should determine the nature of the evaluation or assessment program in spelling. The transfer of words learned in spelling to occasions or situations which demand the correct use of these words is an important objective. It is hardly adequate to get a series of *A's* or 100's on spelling papers if these same words are consistently misspelled in stories, reports, and essays. Thus, a spelling grade, or a report of a child's progress in spelling, should reflect both the child's ability to recall either the appropriate generalization or the correctly memorized series of letters and his ability to use the words he has learned in practical situations. The use of patterns would suggest the appropriateness of testing children's ability to apply pattern generalizations to unfamiliar words. That is, most spelling programs include opportunities for children to exhibit understanding of words they have learned. It would be appropriate to check children's ability to apply a familiar pattern (C-V-C) to words which were perhaps not used in exemplifying the pattern and which may be unfamiliar to them in terms of previous use or "exposure."

Linguists are very critical of our present "functional" spelling programs. They suggest that we do not, in fact, *know* what is functional for various groups of children attending school under widely differing circumstances. They recommend, instead, gradual and sequential introduction to a series of patterns which may be generalized upon to build spelling vocabularies which are inclusive of the great majority of useful words in American English. They favor more reliance upon the stable grapheme-phoneme elements of our language—elements in which a grapheme can be depended upon to represent a specific sound. The regular or stable patterns would be stressed first, then the less regular patterns and the exceptions.

The elementary teacher who wishes to incorporate pattern work into his spelling program may be cautious about abandoning all work which might be considered "functional" or needed for "communication" purposes. Balance seems to be a goal well worth working toward in the spelling program as well as in other areas of the curriculum. It may be difficult but not impossible to work toward the acquisition of a core vocabulary of words which one needs and frequently uses in writing as well as a group of generalizations which can be summoned to help solve the riddle of spelling an unfamiliar word.

Selected References

Allen, Robert, Virginia Allen, and Margaret Shute. *English Sounds and Their Spellings.* New York: Thomas Y. Crowell Co., 1966.

Ames, Wilbur. "A Comparison of Spelling Textbooks." *Elementary English* 42 (1965): 146–52, 188.

Barnhart, Clarence. "Establishing and Maintaining Standard Patterns of Speech." In *Readings in Applied English Linguistics,* edited by Harold Allen, pp. 376–79. New York: Appleton-Century-Crofts, 1958).

Chomsky, Carol. "Invented Spelling in First Grade." Paper presented at Reading Research Institute, June 1974, State University of New York at Buffalo.

Chomsky, Noam, and Morris Halle. *The Sound Pattern of English*. New York: Harper & Row, 1968.

Duckworth, Eleanor. "The Language and Thought of Piaget: Some Comments on Learning to Spell." In *The Language Arts in the Elementary School: A Forum for Focus*, edited by Martha King, Robert Emans, and Patricia Cianciolo, pp. 15–31. Urbana, Ill.: National Council of Teachers of English, 1973.

Hanna, Jean, and Paul Hanna. "Spelling As a School Subject: A Brief History." *The National Elementary School Principal* 38 (1959): 8–23.

Hanna, Paul, Jean Hanna, Richard Hodges, and E. Hugh Rudorf, Jr. *Phoneme-Grapheme Correspondence as Cues to Spelling Improvement*. Washington, D.C.: U.S. Dept. of Health, Education, and Welfare, U.S. Office of Education, 1967.

Hanna, Paul, Richard Hodges, and Jean Hanna. *Spelling: Structure and Strategies*. Boston: Houghton Mifflin Co., 1971.

Hodges, Richard. "The Psychological Bases of Spelling." *Elementary English* 42 (1965): 629–35.

———. "Theoretical Frameworks of English Orthography." *Elementary English* 49 (1972): 1089–97.

Jackson, Gladys. "The Way Out of the Spelling Labyrinth." *Elementary English* 49 (1972): 90–100.

Johnson, Dale, and Edward Merryman. "Syllabication: The Erroneous VCCV Generalization." *Reading Teacher* 26 (1971): 267–70.

Moffett, James. *A Student-Centered Language Arts Curriculum: K-6*. Boston: Houghton Mifflin Co., 1973.

Moffett, James. *Teaching the Universe of Discourse*. Boston: Houghton Mifflin Co., 1973.

Read, Charles. *Children's Categorization of Speech Sounds in English*. Urbana, Ill.: National Council of Teachers of English, 1975.

Read, Charles. "Pre-School Children's Knowledge of English Phonology." *Harvard Educational Review* 41 (1971): 1–34.

Rowell, C. Glennon. "A Prototype for An Individualized Spelling Program." *Elementary English* 49 (1972): 335–40.

Sander, Eric. "Where Are Speech Sounds Learned?" *Journal of Speech and Hearing Disorders* 37 (1972): 55–63.

Sledd, James. *Dictionaries and That Dictionary*. Chicago: Scott Foresman & Co., 1962.

Yee, Albert. "The Generalization Controversy in Spelling Instruction." *Elementary English* 43 (1966): 154–61.

Materials for Children

Children's Dictionaries

My Little Pictionary and *My Second Pictionary* by Marion Monroe and W. Cabell Greet (Chicago: Scott Foresman & Co., 1964, 1970). Introductory books designed to acquaint beginners with the usual arrangement of words in dictionaries as well as to serve as a source book for needed words.

My Picture Dictionary and *My Second Picture Dictionary* by Hale Reid and Helen Crane (Boston: Ginn & Co., 1963, 1967). Also an introductory book, with arrangements by class as well as alphabetically.

Thorndike-Barnhart Beginning Dictionary and *Junior Dictionary* (Chicago: Scott, Foresman & Co., 1974). Dictionaries designed for use in the third or fourth grades through the junior high school grades; lessons in the *use* of these dictionaries are included.

Webster's New Elementary Dictionary (1970) and *Webster's New Practical School Dictionary* (1969) (Springfield, Mass.: G. & C. Merriam Co.). Two dictionaries, each available in a teacher's edition and each containing sequential series of lessons for children and adolescents, designed for use in the third or fourth grades through high school.

With reference to basal spelling programs, it might be noted that several publishers use the term *linguistic* in their advertising; when one views their materials, however, one finds a rather unsatisfactory compromise between utility, or function, and structure. Therefore, a listing of spelling series has been omitted. Rather, classroom teachers are encouraged to look at new material very carefully, apply the criteria for linguistic programs suggested in this chapter, and select the program or basal series which comes closest to meeting the needs of the pupils they teach.

4

Linguistics and the Teaching of Grammar and Usage

Raven McDavid writes: "Language . . . is a system of arbitrary vocal symbols by which a social group cooperate and interact and transmit their culture."[1]

Judith Greene defines *language* as "the infinite set of grammatical sentences in a language." She defines *grammar* as "a finite set of rules that will generate this infinite set of grammatical sentences and no nonsentences."[2]

Three grammatical theories will be dealt with in this chapter; Greene contends that these grammars can, and should, be judged on the basis of observational adequacy, descriptive adequacy, and explanatory adequacy. (Only transformational-generative grammars meet all three criteria, since the criteria are almost wholly based upon this theory.)

Noam Chomsky, whose name is preeminent among transformational-generative grammarians, writes:

Each grammar is a theory of a particular language, specifying formal and semantic properties of an infinite array of sentences. These sentences, each with its particular structure, constitute the language generated by the grammar. The languages so generated are those that can be "learned" in a normal way. The language faculty,

---

1. Raven McDavid, Jr., "The Cultural Matrix of American English," *Elementary English* 42 (1965): 15.

2. Judith Greene, *Psycholinguistics: Chomsky and Psychology* (Harmondsworth, Middlesex, England: Penguin Books, 1972), p. 34.

given appropriate stimulation, will construct a grammar; the person knows the language generated by the constructed grammar. This knowledge can then be used to understand what is heard and to produce discourse as in expression of thought within the constraints of the internalized principles, in a manner appropriate to situations as these are conceived by other mental faculties, free of stimulus control.[3]

Chafe conceives of "language as a system linking meaning with sound."[4] This belief, leading to what has been termed *case grammar* or *generative semantics,* differs from transformational grammar in several significant respects.

In this chapter, these three major approaches to the study of grammar will be compared and contrasted, and, perhaps of more importance to the reader, the issue of whether or not instruction in grammar is appropriate, or meaningful, for elementary school pupils will be discussed.

There are a few principles which apply to all languages. These should be listed and amplified prior to a discussion of grammar or grammars.

Language is Arbitrary

There is nothing about a chair which requires that it be called a chair. A piece of furniture with legs, a seat, and a back is called a chair, and when the back is removed the name is changed to stool. These decisions are arbitrary and the result of some conventions agreed upon by those who speak the English language. A very brief summary of the most significant developments in the evolution of the English language was included in the first chapter of this book. It was noted that the choice of a Norman-French term (*beef*) for a type of meat rather than an Anglo-Saxon term (*cow*) was motivated by a desire to please and imitate the conquerers of the British Isles, but it was a choice. Neither term is ordained, nor is one superior to the other. When a self-contained apparatus, designed to hold humans as they are hurled into space, was developed, the term *capsule* was applied, and this term took on an additional meaning. When technicians developed an undersea vehicle, a new word was coined: *sub,* suggesting *under* and *mar*ine, connoting *water,* from *mare,* the Latin word for *sea. Television* has a similar history of coinage: a Latin word (*video,* meaning *to look* or *see*) with a Greek prefix (*tele,* meaning *distant*). The point is that new products, new inventions, and changes in our political or social structure require the invention of new words and changes or shifts in the meanings of other words.

Changes also occur which result in the discarding of words from our language—we seldom speak of *parlors* or *cellars* in modern homes. Refrigerators have generally replaced iceboxes. The claim that our language is arbitrary, that it changes in response to human needs, can hardly be considered controversial. Once this is pointed out to an elementary teacher, the response is likely to be, "That's true. . . ." When, however, one suggests that "It is me" is replacing "It is I" as acceptable usage, and that *whom* is fast disappearing from our language, then the matter of

3. Noam Chomsky, *Reflections on Language* (New York: Pantheon Books, 1975), p. 13.
4. Wallace Chafe, *Meaning and the Structure of Language* (Chicago: University of Chicago Press, 1970), p. 2.

arbitrariness becomes more controversial. Isn't this an abandonment of all standards? Doesn't the elementary teacher, especially, have the responsibility of maintaining "high standards" in spoken and written communication? No, neither the elementary teacher nor anyone else has this responsibility. Linguistics has been defined as the scientific study of language; linguists are *students* of change, of language as it once was and/or as it is now. Neither the linguist nor anyone else sets standards for American English nor do linguists attempt to decide what is or is not "correct." The arbitrary nature of language suggests that change is normal, that language standards vary from one group or social class to another and with reference to different situations. All linguists attempt to do is to point out as standard English those patterns which are currently used by most educated speakers of a language. It is this standard that elementary teachers should stress.

Language Is Conventional

It would do little good for an individual to determine that *chair* is a foolish word and that *darsk* is a much better one and henceforth to use the term she has invented. It would do little good for an individual to do this because she will on occasion have need to communicate this term with another human being, who would not understand her. Unless a body of words and the conventions for organizing these words into phrases, sentences, and paragraphs are shared in common by the members of a linguistic group (a basic purpose for which language exists), communication cannot exist. Not only must the words, or groups of phonemes and morphemes, convey meaning but so must the suprasegmental phonemes which have already been mentioned. A rise in pitch at the end of an utterance indicates that it is a question[5] or at least that a response is expected. Juncture, or pause, especially at an unexpected place, causes us to listen with more than usual care for what is coming next.

A language must include a system of conventions, or those who speak and write it cannot communicate. It might be noted here that these conventions change and that it is for this reason that the arbitrary nature of language is listed first. To identify something as *tough* communicates one thing to an adolescent who uses the current idiomatic expressions easily and correctly; the same term communicates something else to a waitress or a chef in a restaurant to whom you are complaining about a piece of meat. Most American English conventions regarding word order are accepted by almost all the speakers of the language. In addition, there are conventions which add depth and simplify communication among members of an occupational or a social group. Conventions shared by small subgroups serve the purpose of excluding outsiders and identifying those who "belong"—the term *pedagese* has been coined to categorize the professional terminology of teachers. *Accountability, competence,* and *open concept* are terms used by many groups, but these have a very specialized meanings for teachers and school administrators.

---

5. "You're going home now" is a statement if there is strong stress on *home* and a fall in pitch on *now*. It becomes a question if there is a rise in pitch on the word *now*. This is one factor which makes our traditional classifications of types of sentences so misleading!

Language Is Culturally Transmitted

There are two important points to be made with respect to this characteristic. We learn our language, in part at least, by listening to those who speak it—well or poorly.

Dialect, a subset of a language, or a variety of language which does not *seriously* impede communication with other speakers of that language, varies from social class to social class. A child who comes to school using nonstandard grammar may well be penalized in terms of educational advancement, social acceptance (outside the "circles" in which she now moves), and occupational opportunity. It is for this reason, not because "She done it" is *wrong,* that teachers will try to help children, especially inner-city or culturally different children, (1) develop several languages and (2) learn to choose the variety of language most appropriate for the situation.

To illustrate this problem in professional, adult terms, consider the manner in which you would ask for cream for coffee in the following circumstances:

—in the teacher's lounge or in a quick "recess" coffee break
—at home, at a meal with one's family
—at a reception for the new superintendent of schools
—at dinner in the home of some wealthy and influential school patrons
—when being interviewed for a new teaching position, a position which is very desirable

Culturally different children are not alone in needing and utilizing a variety of language patterns, from informal language to language chosen very carefully to please and impress. Such children may need help in adding to their dialects language patterns that will not unduly hinder their social acceptance or inhibit professional or educational progress.

It is worth reemphasizing the premise that helping a child select more acceptable language should not be accompanied by rejection of the language the child presently uses. If we communicate to a child by gesture, facial expression, or disapproving words that *her* language is unacceptable, the child may feel somewhat unacceptable and unworthy. No teacher of the language arts wishes to impede or stand in the way of improved communications, yet, all too often, this is what happens. A teacher's negative attitude toward nonstandard dialect may well be one of the most influential factors impeding a child's acquisition of standard dialect, although this is certainly not the teacher's intent.

Language Is a Highly Complicated Structure
Containing Many Strands or Facets

As an example of the complex nature of American English, note the following group of nonsense syllables. The structural meaning of these words is clear, although the lexical meaning is obscure.

The bingest sturks were stingled by a klunny bung retingly.

Only *the, by, a,* and *were* have a clear lexical and structural meaning. Much more can be known about this sentence if the structural meaning is analyzed. *The* clues the reader (or listener) to the fact that *sturks* is a noun. *A* does the same thing for *bung*. It seems clear that *bingest* and *klunny* are adjectives describing *sturks* and *bung,* respectively. "The bingest sturks" might be "the largest boys" or "the happiest girls." A "klunny bung" might be a "skinny bird" or a "sunny day." *Retingly* suggests the manner in which the klunny bung stingled the bingest sturks; *retingly* is the "freest" word in the sentence; it could make structural sense in any of several positions. It is particularly appropriate in either the initial or final "slots" of the sentence. This is characteristic of an adverb or adverbial clause. Few speakers of American English would have any trouble identifying *sturks* as plural, and *bung* as singular; "were stingled by" obviously suggests passive voice.

Part of the complexity of American English, then, results from the difficulty of determining the lexical and the structural significance of a word. At the risk of being redundant, it could be pointed out that, as with sounds, meaning cannot be clearly determined or prescribed when a word is viewed in isolation. Fill in the blanks in the following sentences. (Note, as the sentences are completed, the pronunciation shifts.)

Please _____ the _____ of her performance
in this meet. \ri-'kȯrd\, \'rek-ərd\

In the sentence above, the same letter sequence assumes different positions, the structural meanings change from verb to noun, and pronunciation changes. Stress moves from the second syllable to the first.

_____ my sore back with an alcohol _____.
\'rəb\ or (rub).

In this sentence, the same word assumes a different lexical meaning, and the structural meaning changes from verb to noun. The pronunciation is not affected in this case.

It is of somewhat limited value, therefore, to ask a child to define *record* or *rub* out of context, unless multiple definitions, both lexical and structural, are acceptable.

The four principles which have been explained in some detail are basic to any discussion of the implications of linguistic science for teaching grammar and usage in the elementary school. In fact, these are basic linguistic principles which underlie most of the linguists' recommendations for changing practices in teaching the language arts.

Grammar Defined

Grammar, as typically defined by language scholars, is not prescriptive and is not intended to indicate that which is acceptable as contrasted to that which is unacceptable. Nor is grammar the proper title for a curricular area or subdivision of English designed to cause children to speak and write more "correctly." The story of the boy who wrote on the chalkboard, "Dear Teacher: I have wrote 'I have gone' one hundred times, like you said, and I have went home" is a well-known cliché exemplifying the futility of much of the instruction in grammar and usage in the past.

If grammar is *not* each of these things, what then is it? Robert Pooley defines grammar as "a description of the way we speak and write English."[6] Paul Roberts defines grammar as "something that produces the sentences of a language, whether the something is a book or a machine, or a human being who speaks the language natively."[7] W. Nelson Francis provides not one, but three definitions of grammar. All three are included here because the differences Francis discusses may help to dispel some of the misconceptions which exist about grammar.

> The first thing we mean by "grammar" is "the set of formal patterns in which the words of a language are arranged in order to convey larger meanings. It is not necessary that we be able to discuss these patterns self consciously in order to be able to use them. In fact, all speakers of any language above the age of five or six know how to use its complex forms of organization with considerable skill, in this sense of the word—call it "Grammar 1"—they are thoroughly familiar with its grammar.
>
> The second meaning of "grammar"—call it "Grammar 2"—is the branch of linguistic science which is concerned with the description, analysis, and formalization of formal language patterns . . . grammar in the first sense was in operation before anyone formulated the first rule that began the history of grammar as a study.
>
> The third sense in which people use the word "grammar" is "linguistic etiquette." This we may call "Grammar 3." The word in this sense is often coupled with a derogatory adjective; the expression "He ain't there" is "bad grammar." What we mean is that such an expression is bad linguistic manners, in certain circles.

Francis concludes:

> These then, are the three meanings of grammar: Grammar 1, a form of behavior; Grammar 2, a field of study, a science; and Grammar 3, a branch of etiquette.[8]

The elementary teacher would be well advised to recognize the basic and pervasive nature of Grammar 1, to apprise himself of the findings related to Grammar 2, and to be wary of using Grammar 3 as a punitive device for pupils or as a series of entrance requirements to a club so exclusive that most adults, including English teachers, would not qualify for membership.

What Grammar Should Be Taught?

In the chapter concerned with spelling and the implications of linguistic research for spelling programs in elementary schools, it was pointed out that there was some controversy regarding the "stability" or general applicability of three, or four, or eight basic spelling patterns. Research findings appeared to be contradictory, and the advice was given to use spelling patterns where they obviously apply and in cases in which children can easily make generalizations which lead to independence and self-confidence in spelling. The same procedure may be helpful in ana-

---

6. Robert Pooley, "What About Grammar?" in *Readings In The Language Arts In The Elementary School,* ed. James MacCampbell (Boston: D. C. Heath & Co., 1964), p. 21.
7. Paul Roberts, *English Sentences* (New York: Harcourt Brace Jovanovich, 1962), p. 17.
8. Nelson Francis, "Revolution in Grammar," in *Readings in Applied English Linguistics,* 2nd ed., ed. Harold Allen (New York: Appleton-Century-Crofts, 1964), pp. 69, 70.

lyzing the linguists' findings in the area of grammar and the implications of these findings for language programs in elementary schools.

The Role of Traditional Grammar

The reader may recall, as a pupil, "English" programs which consisted largely of the following components:

1. Memorization of parts of speech and their definitions. "A noun is the name of a person, place, or thing." Does this include such abstractions as *freedom, democracy,* and *beauty*? In fact, isn't such a definition an enumeration rather than a definition? *Noun,* in fact, means *name,* doesn't it?

   The definition of a verb as an "action word" gets one into even more trouble. Where does this leave forms of the verb *to be?* Even broadening the definition to include "state of being" is not much more helpful. State of being appears to be more applicable to nouns like *health and happiness* than to a verb form like *is* or *was.* The term *action word,* which might include *action, "running,"* and various other nonverbs, is clearly inadequate· as a definition of a verb.

2. The division of stiff, unnatural sentences into categories named by the parts of speech listed above. For example: "The father of the child watched from the window" is diagrammed as follows:

   The simple sentence is "father (noun) watched (verb)." "Of the child" is a prepositional phrase used as an adjective; "from the window" is a prepositional phrase used as an adverb.

   Aside from the questionable utility of a series of definitions like those above, it does not seem that this particular method of diagramming helps a child to see the basic "building blocks" of a sentence more clearly.

3. "Filling in the blanks" to indicate one's understanding of the use of singular, plural, agreement of persons, and so forth.

> They _____ coming home for lunch.
>   (is, are)
>
> She _____ have the tickets, I'm afraid.
>   (don't, doesn't)

Exercises of this type probably do not accomplish very much in terms of improving children's usage. In fact, one might seriously question the significance of all the components mentioned so far.

Traditional grammar, then, is criticized on several counts: it fails to describe its operations with any consistency, it depends upon some understanding of terms such as the parts of speech before real study of the components of a sentence can begin, and, finally, it has failed to have much impact on composition or even on speech, which is more basic. Of course, it fails to meet any of Judith Greene's criteria.

Traditional English grammars had their origins in the Renaissance and were largely imitative of the Latin grammars then in existence. Latin grammars were copied because Latin was considered such a "perfect language." Today, linguists are prone to speak in less than complimentary terms of "latinate grammars." Their claim is that a grammar which adequately described Latin cannot adequately describe a different language such as English. On this issue, Wilson writes:

> At the outset these English grammars were neither very accurate nor very efficient; they were usually attempts to find in English the equivalents of forms and construction which could be found in Latin, or failing that, to insist that such forms be developed and that English grammar be corrected and improved to meet that standard. This side of traditional grammars—their reforming zeal in the effort to make English grammar conform to the system of Latin grammar—we usually call prescriptive because these grammarians attempted to prescribe what English should be rather than to describe what it currently was.[9]

Many, but not all, traditional grammarians are *prescriptive* rather than *descriptive*. Enough has already been said about the dangers of a prescriptive grammar which tells (or attempts to tell) people how to speak and write. Such grammars operate from a false assumption—that there is a standard English grammar which is changeless and that the school's task is to develop competence in understanding its elements by using methods and techniques already described.

Traditional grammars—descriptive, not prescriptive—have been called "circular": an English sentence can be described only after the total meaning of the sentence is understood. When a sentence is classified as a statement or question, its components can then be described and their relationships analyzed. Traditional grammars have been criticized for this quality of "analyzing from the outside." Traditional grammarians describe English with great detail, a necessary characteristic since traditionalists must work from specific sentences and cannot help in the development of principles for the organization of sentences not yet spoken or written.

In other words, just as traditional approaches to the teaching of spelling often fail to help with the spelling of unfamiliar words, traditional approaches to the teaching of grammar, in addition to being somewhat ineffective and prescriptive, too often force reliance upon detailed analysis of artificial sentences.

What Is a Sentence?

Before discussing the contributions of linguists to grammar programs in elementary schools (the other grammars, structural, transformational, and case, which

---

9. Kenneth Wilson, "English Grammars and the Grammar of English," in *Teachers Notebook,* ed. A Segal (New York: Harcourt Brace Jovanovich, 1964).

they suggest as replacements for traditional grammar), it would be wise to come to an understanding of what a sentence is. This may seem to be a simple matter— subject and predicate; noun, verb, and their modifiers—each of these memorized definitions can be recalled, if painfully. As a matter of fact, the problems of defining a sentence are not simple ones at all; how are sentences like "Oh!" "Ouch!" or "Heavens!" accounted for by definitions like those memorized by many elementary children and included in many language texts? Paul Roberts writes:

> We could say that a sentence is "a group of words expressing a complete thought" or "a group of words that begins with a capital letter and ends with a period. But obviously these definitions do not get us very far. We want answers to questions such as these: "Just what groups of English words express complete thoughts?" "Just what groups of words are written with a capital letter at the beginning and a period at the end?"[10]

Definitions of sentences may concentrate on meaning (a complete thought) or function (a sentence is a structure in a language which is not shown by some grammatical feature to be part of a larger structure). David Crystal writes:

> "Sentence" refers to certain features of language and not others. Exactly where the boundary line is to be drawn between what constitutes a sentence and what does not is to a very great extent a matter of definition. . . . In one model, there may be a distinction made between 'sentence' and 'clause', let us say; another model may decide not to talk about clauses at all, referring to them as types of sentences; a third may even try to do without the term 'sentence', talking instead of 'utterance' or some such notion. Any one of these approaches could be illuminating, and could, if developed sufficiently, produce an organized account of grammatical phenomena which is comprehensive, self-consistent, and intuitively satisfying . . . no grammatical theory has achieved any of these aims . . . we can only demand explicitness in people's use of the term, and take pains to understand any given definition in the light of the theory as a whole of which it constitutes a part.[11]

Although there are significant units larger than a sentence, Crystal concludes that "the sentence is the largest unit recognized by the linguist as being capable of accounting for the range of grammatical classes and structures which turn up in a language."[12] The issues surrounding the tendency of some grammarians to limit their field of analysis to the sentence are many, complex, and cannot be dealt with adequately by this author in this text. Noting that "sentences are a rather small part of language," Robinson writes:

> The sentence must be used in language: hence Chomsky's effort to describe sentences by rules which are those of the whole language. But Chomsky's concentration on isolated sentences is itself a kind of atomism, for the sentence, to be a sentence, needs a home in language as well as in the rules of syntax, it needs a situation which will allow it to do what it does in a sentence.[13]

---

10. Paul Roberts, *English Syntax* (New York: Harcourt Brace Jovanovich, 1964), p. 1.
11. David Crystal, *Linguistics* (Harmondsworth, Middlesex, England: Penguin Books, 1970), p. 200.
12. Ibid., p. 201.
13. Ian Robinson, *The New Grammarians' Funeral* (Cambridge: At the University Press, 1975), p. 45.

Gleason concludes:

> The sentence is probably undefinable, short of a very extensive set of statements—
> a whole grammar, in fact. Yet this should not dismay anyone. Few basic grammatical
> concepts can be defined easily. It would seem best to abandon the attempt, and to
> apply the effort to more promising endeavors.[14]

In the case of this present endeavor, the effort will now be applied to attempting
to establish some useful distinctions between structural grammar, transformational-
generative grammar, and case grammar.

The Role of Structural Grammar

Structuralists talk and write in terms of sentence patterns, not to be confused with
the phoneme-grapheme patterns described in chapter 3 (except that both operate
sequentially and proceed from the simple to the complex). Not all structural linguists group sentences as the following patterns suggest, but this is a common and
widely used sequence developed by Paul Roberts.[15]

Pattern I

This is the simplest pattern, and it consists of a noun and a verb with the possible
addition of a determiner:

SUBJECT		PREDICATE		
(Determiner)	*Noun or Pronoun*	*Verb-intransitive*	+	*(Adverb)*
(The)[16]	girl	plays		(nicely)
(The)	dogs	bark		(loudly)

Determiner may be a new term to the reader. This class of words includes
articles (*a, an, the*), possessives (*my, your, its*), and demonstratives (*this, that,
these, those*).

Determiners occur with nouns, but certain determiners (*both, many, few, several*)
will occur only with plural nouns (*women, people*), while others (*each, every, a,
an*) occur only with singular nouns (*woman, person*).

Pattern I is a pattern with wide utility; it is the intransitive verb which helps to
distinguish it from Pattern II.

Helping Children with Pattern I. Children can be helped to understand Pattern I
through the completion of exercises similar to the following:

A. Write five examples of Pattern I, like "Girls run," or "Boys run swiftly."

B. List five intransitive verbs (verbs which can occur in Pattern I).

---

14. Henry Gleason, Jr., *Linguistics and English Grammar* (New York: Holt, Rinehart &
Winston, 1965), p. 330.
15. Roberts, *English Sentences,* portions of chapters 4–8, summarized on pp. 50–51.
16. Parentheses in the discussion of this pattern and succeeding patterns indicate that tne
class may or may not occur.

C. List five verb-adverb combinations (*come in,* etc.).

D. Change the form of the following verbs:

simple	*-s*	*ed*	*ing*
play			
bark			
look			
snow			
fill			

After the basic pattern has been introduced (and patterns of verb parts demonstrated or, better still, discovered inductively), the pattern can be altered by the process of coordination without changing the basic pattern.

Boys and girls run swiftly and surely.

In Pattern I sentences, both the noun and the verb can be compounded by the use of a coordinating conjunction or coordinator (*and, or; either, or; both, and*).

It is important for children to recognize in dealing with Pattern I sentences that a coordinator in the predicate usually connects only the last two words.

The girls jumped, ran, and played.

Pattern II

SUBJECT		PREDICATE	
(Determiner)	*Noun or Pronoun*	*Verb (Linking)*	*Adjective*
(The)	boys	seem	handsome
(Some)	girls	appear	lazy

Other examples of the differences between Patterns I and II follow.

The boy grows fast. (Pattern I)
The boy seemed fast. (Pattern II)

The girl grew quickly. (Pattern I)
The girl grew tall. (Pattern II)

Much of the work with children will be in terms of distinguishing these patterns, including the possible ambiguities.

Helping Children with Pattern II. Exercises similar to the following may be helpful in developing children's understanding of Pattern II:

A. Identify the following sentences as Pattern I or Pattern II.

1. The girl dressed beautifully. (I)
2. The girl looked beautiful. (II)

1. The carpenter worked hard. (I)
2. The carpenter seemed hard. (II)

1. The boy went away. (I)
2. The woman seemed tall. (II)

B. What other words can add to these descriptions? (continuing the principle of coordinates)

   1. The man seemed tall and _____.
                            (thin, scrawny, muscular)

   2. The girl looked beautiful but _____.
                            (sad, unhappy)

   3. The girl grew tall and _____.
                            (lovely, beautiful)

C. Change the forms of the verbs in the following sentences without changing the basic meaning of the sentences.
   1. The work does seem hard.
   2. (The work seems hard.)

   1. The girl does look beautiful.
   2. (The girl looks beautiful.)

   1. The boy will grow tall.
   2. (The boy grows tall.)

D. What words would be appropriate to complete the following sentences?
   1. It smelled _____.
   2. Roses smell _____.
   3. He felt _____.
   4. The milk tasted _____.
   5. She remained _____.

Now, check each of the sentences you have just completed. Are they Pattern I or Pattern II?

Pattern III

SUBJECT			PREDICATE	
(Determiner)	*Noun-Pronoun*	*Verb (of the "become" or "remain" class)*	*(Determiner)*	*Noun*
(The)	boy	becomes	a	man
(The)	girl	remained	my	friend
(The)	milk	became		cheese

It is clear that there are not too many sentences following this pattern. It is one pattern which has no special classification in traditional grammar, and the "became" or "becomes" verbs have no special name (linking, transitive, and so forth).

Helping Children with Pattern III. Exercises such as these may help children understand Pattern III:

A. Complete these sentences, making sure that a *noun* fills the last position. ("The man remained friendly" would be an example of another pattern—which one?)

   1. The dog remained _____.
                     (his pet?)

   2. The girl became _____.
                     (a teenager?)

   3. Father remained _____.
                     (a helper?)

B. From the following sentences, identify those which are Pattern I, Pattern II, and Pattern III.

   1. Susan became my friend. (III)
   2. The milk became ice cream. (III)
   3. The shipment arrived and was unloaded. (I)
   4. That happened quickly. (I)
   5. It smells good. (II)
   6. Steve became my friend and my neighbor. (III)

Pattern IV

SUBJECT		PREDICATE		
(Determiner)	*Noun*	*Verb-transitive*	*(Determiner)*	*Noun*
(The)	woman	ate	(her)	dinner
(The)	girl	shot	(the)	fox
(The)	nurse	helped		Edith

The noun or pronoun in the predicate in Pattern IV is called an object. This marks the essential difference between Patterns III and IV.

          Pattern III: Susan became my friend.

          Pattern IV: Susan helped my friend.

In the Pattern III sentence, *Susan* and *friend* refer to the same person; in the Pattern IV sentence, they do not.

Helping Children with Pattern IV. The following exercises may help chlidren gain some understanding of Pattern IV sentences:

A. Identify the following sentences as examples of Pattern III or Pattern IV.

   1. John remained my tutor. (III)
   2. John accompanied my tutor. (IV)
   3. Betty became my wife. (III)
   4. Betty liked my wife. (IV)

B. Complete the following sentences. Decide whether the completed sentence is an example of Pattern III or Pattern IV.

   1. The girl paid _____.
                (the check, the bill)

2. Juanita found _____.
       (her father, Bill)
3. The boy hid _____.
       (his money, his books)
4. The story pleased _____.
       (us, them)
5. The building cost _____.
       (money, $500,000)

Pattern V

SUBJECT			PREDICATE			
(Determiner)	*Noun or Pronoun*	*Verb (of the "give" class)*	*(Determiner)*	*Noun*	*(Determiner)*	*Noun*
(The)	woman	gave	(her)	son	(a)	car
	I	gave		him	(some)	money
	Mary	brought	(her)	mother	(some)	flowers

Children can discover that the first noun in the predicate (*son, him, mother*) is an indirect object, and the second noun in the predicate (*car, money, flowers*) is a direct object.

Helping Children with Pattern V. These exercises are examples of those which might help children understand Pattern V sentences:

A. Please complete the following sentences, making certain they conform to Pattern V.

1. The girl _____ her mother the _____.
          (gave)   (book)
2. The pupil _____ his teacher the _____.
          (brought)   (report card)
3. Mother _____ her son his _____.
          (brought)   (coat)
4. The aunt _____ her niece the _____.
          (gave)   (gift)

Which words in the sentences above are direct objects of the verb? Which are the indirect objects?

Pattern VI

SUBJECT			PREDICATE		
(Determiner)	*Noun*	*Verb (of the "consider" class)*	*Noun*	*(Determiner)*	*Noun*
(My)	sister	considered	me	(a)	fool
(My)	father	thought	me	(a)	scholar

In Pattern V, the two nouns or pronoun and noun in the predicate refer to different things (*son–car; him–money; mother–flowers*). In Pattern VI, they refer to the same things (*me*-a *fool; me*-a *scholar*). In this pattern, the first noun or pronoun in the predicate is an object, the second is usually called an object complement. Pattern VI also includes variations of the sentences above, as follows:

> My sister considered me foolish.
> My father thought me scholarly.

(The change here is the substitution of an adjective for a second noun.)

Helping Children with Pattern VI. These exercises may help children in understanding sentences of Pattern VI:

A. Read each of the following sentences and decide whether they are examples of Pattern V or Pattern VI:

   1. The teacher gave the boy a book. (V)
   2. The teacher considered my sister an honest girl. (VI)
   3. The parents brought their children gifts. (V)
   4. The parents believed their children geniuses. (VI)

Change each of the Pattern VI sentences above so that an adjective replaces the second noun.

Pattern VII

SUBJECT		PREDICATE		
(*Determiner*)	*Noun*	*Verb* (*of the* "*elect*" *class*)	(*Determiner*) *Noun*	(*Determiner*) *Noun*
	They	chose	(my) sister	president
	We	elected	John	chairman
(The)	class	voted	her	(the) leader

These sentences are not markedly different from Pattern VI sentences. One difference is that an adjective cannot be substituted for the second noun. In both patterns, however, the last noun serves as an object complement, and in both patterns the nouns or pronouns in the predicate refer to the same person or thing.

Helping Children with Pattern VII. The following exercises may be helpful to children in gaining an understanding of Pattern VII sentences:

A. Complete these sentences, following the description provided for Pattern VII sentences.

   1. _____ elected Bob _____.
      (He, We)   (chairman, secretary)

   2. _____ chose her _____.
      (The class, They)   (monitor, queen)

   3. _____ appointed him _____.
      (The mayor, The governor)   (chief, secretary)

The following three patterns, Patterns VIII through X, all use as the verb *be* or a *be* form. Exercises for children will follow descriptions and examples of the three patterns.

Pattern VIII

SUBJECT		PREDICATE	
(Determiner)	*Noun*	*Verb (of the "be" class)*	*Adverb*
(The)	girl	was	here
(The)	boy	is	there

Although there are similarities to Pattern I, there are significant differences as well:

1. The verb is of the *be* class (*be, am, are, is, was, were, being, been*).
2. The adverb must occur in this pattern. The addition of *there* provides a variation of this pattern; Pattern VIII would include "There was a boy here" as well as the example given above, "The girl was here."

Pattern IX

SUBJECT		PREDICATE	
(Determiner)	*Noun*	*Verb (of the "be" class)*	*Adjective*
	She	was	tired
	He	was	hungry
	Mary	is	pretty

Although it is similar to Pattern II, Pattern IX is much more commonly used. One difference is the manner in which negatives are formed. She was *not* tired (Pattern IX). The boys *do not* seem handsome (Pattern II).

Pattern X

SUBJECT		PREDICATE		
(Determiner)	*Noun*	*Verb (of the "be" class)*	*(Determiner)*	*Noun*
	Susan	was	(my)	sponsor
	Mary	is	(my)	friend

Pattern X is much more common than Pattern III, which it closely resembles. Differences are similar to those identified between Pattern II and Pattern IX. It will be noted that, as in Pattern III, the two nouns or noun and pronoun refer to the same thing or person.

Helping Children with Patterns VIII through X. These exercises are designed to help children distinguish among the last three patterns and compare and contrast them with the similar patterns introduced earlier.

A. Classify these sentences as examples of Patterns VIII, IX, or X:

    1. Mary is angry. (IX)
    2. She was here. (VIII)
    3. The teacher is my friend. (X)
    4. The class was noisy. (IX)

B. Match the following *be* sentences with the sentences they resemble which represent Patterns I, II, or III. (The *be* verbs are italicized.)

The boy became my friend. (Pattern III)
    2. The class *is* busy. (Pattern IX)
    3. The class worked hard. (Pattern I)
    4. The boy grew tall. (Pattern II)
    5. The girl *is* my friend. (Pattern X)
    6. Mary *is* outside. (Pattern VIII)

C. Write three sentences to illustrate Pattern VIII, three to illustrate Pattern IX, and three to illustrate Pattern X.

It should be *restated* that this brief description of the basic sentence patterns of English is not the only description developed by structuralists. Because other approaches to grammar are currently more highly regarded by linguists, no other examples of a structural approach will be considered here. It is probably true that most textbook series still utilize this approach.

Structural grammar, according to Ralph Goodman, "attempts to give rules for automatically analyzing arbitrarily given sentences,"[17] That is, patterns, whether three, four, five, or ten, are provided as models for the analysis of existing sentences. Structural grammar is based upon spoken sentences in American English, and for this reason, if no other, it represents a step forward from the traditional "latinate" grammar to which most readers (and this writer) were exposed as elementary school pupils. It is *not* the purpose of structural grammar, as an approach to teaching and learning syntax, to teach pupils to decompose sentences more efficiently.

There have been serious criticisms of the concern for working with units no longer than the sentence by transformational grammarians. Robinson writes:

Sentences are a rather small part of language. Chomsky never gives any account of paragraphs, chapters, books or any of the larger units of which sentences are a kind of atom. But it is the larger unit which decides what the sentence is doing in language, not vice versa.[18]

---

17. Ralph Goodman, "Transformational Grammar," in *An Introductory English Grammar,* ed. Norman Stageburg (New York: Holt, Rinehart & Winston, 1965).
18. Robinson, *The New Grammarians' Funeral,* p. 45.

Chafe explains:

> Syntactic description has usually taken the sentence to be its basic unit of organiza-
> tion, although probably no one would deny that systematic constraints exist across
> sentence boundaries as well. From time to time attention has been given to a dis-
> course structure, but the structure of the sentence has seemed to exhibit a kind of
> closure which allows it to be investigated in relative, if not complete, inde-
> pendence.[19]

Chafe's position will be further explained in the section of the chapter which deals
with case grammar.

Transformational Grammar

This is, perhaps, the logical point for moving to a brief discussion of transformational grammar. Perhaps the major contrastive feature between structural grammar
and transformational grammar is the fact that transformational grammar is *generative,* that is, transformational grammar purports to provide *rules* for producing new
sentences as well as *patterns* for the analysis of existing sentences. Although sentence
patterns are suggested in transformational grammars, these serve a different function than they do in structural grammars.

Transformational grammar is based upon a series of rules or a set of directions
for producing or generating sentences. The term *transformational* refers to the
division of American English sentences into two classifications: (1) basic sentences
and (2) the transforms, or variations, of these basic sentences. The basic or kernel
sentence is composed of two parts, the noun phrase and the verb phrase. The
formula for a basic sentence might be written as follows:

Sentence → Noun Phrase + Verb Phrase (S → NP + VP)[20]

The noun phrase and the verb phrase may each consist of only one word. In the
sentence "Boys play," for example, the noun phrase is *Boys,* the verb phrase is
play. This sentence might be diagrammed as follows:

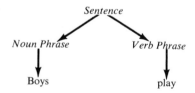

Notice that the diagram above begins with the "directions" or "rules" for rewriting,
rather than representing an arbitrary division of an existing group of words (sentence) into its component parts.

Further explanation is in order if the formula suggested above is to account for a

---

19. Chafe, *Meaning and the Structure of Language,* p. 95.
20. Sentence may be rewritten as a noun phrase + a verb phrase.

variety of sentence types or patterns discussed in the preceding section of this chapter (the section dealing with structural grammar). Patterns have been suggested by several linguists who are generally considered transformationalists, and these patterns do not differ a great deal from those described previously. Mellon terms his patterns "basic sentence types," and he lists five of these:

1. The Intransitive-Verb Sentence
   The boy arrived.
2. The Transitive-Verb Object Sentence
   The boy remained a dunce.
3. The Transitive-Verb or Object Sentence
   The boy frightened his sister.
4. The Have Sentence
   The boy has a bicycle.
5. The Be Sentence
   The boy is intelligent.
   The boy is a scholar.
   The boy is in school.[21]

Ralph Goodman contrasts the structural patterns listed by Stageburg with his own transformational patterns. He notes one pattern which Stageburg considers a pattern but which transformationalists do not:

1. *N   V (be)   Adj.*
   Food   is   good

2. *N   V (be)   Uninflected Word*
   The girl is   here

3. *N   V   N*
   My brother is a doctor

4. *N   Intransitive Verb (In V)*
   Girls   giggle

5. *N   Transitive Verb (Tr V)   N*
   The girls   bought   the dress

6. *N   Tr. V   N   N*
   Mother   bought the girl a dress

7. *N   Tr. V N^2 N^2*
   The players chose   Harry   a captain   (Goodman indicates that no. 7 is *not* considered a basic pattern in transformational grammar.)

8. *N   Linking Verb (LV)   Adj.*
   The acrobat   seems   young

9. *N   LV   N*
   My brother   remained an outstanding student[22]

---

21. John Mellon, *The Basic Sentence Types and Their Simple Transforms* (Culver, Ind.: Culver Military Academy, 1964), p. 51.
22. Goodman, "Transformational Grammar," p. 293.

Linguists can and do point out striking differences between the structural and the transformational approaches to syntax. The differences which appear to be of some significance to the work of the elementary teacher seem to be the following:

1. Structural grammar provides patterns for categorizing existing sentences, while transformational grammar provides rules or directions which are applicable to sentences as yet unspoken or unwritten.
2. The patterns which are used in transformational grammar are helpful in describing sentences which have been generated, but they do not serve the "basic" function that patterns serve in structural grammar.
3. The tree diagram and the formula $S \rightarrow NP + VP$ is illustrative of the transformationalists' claim that theirs is a more scientific approach to the study of syntax.

If the tree diagram reminds the reader of similar devices used in the classification of plants or animals in a botany or zoology class, this is not coincidental but is precisely what linguists of the transformationalist school of thought intend. They are eager and anxious to move language from a "pseudo-scientific science" to a "science." It would be appropriate at this point to explore somewhat more fully the terms *noun phrase* and *verb phrase,* since these terms are basic to the transformationalists' sentence formula, and the detailing of the noun phrase and verb phrase provides most of the "branches" on the tree diagrams. Sentence → Noun Phrase + Verb Phrase ($S \rightarrow NP + VP$) is the basic formula:

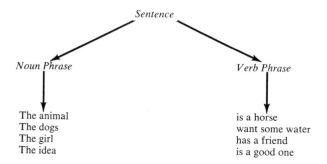

The Noun Phrase

In the noun phrases listed above, each phrase consists of a determiner[23] and a noun. Elimination of the determiner from the noun phrase makes the resulting sentence ungrammatical. Number (singular or plural)—*girl, dogs*—also plays a major role in the makeup or organization of a noun phrase. The following, then, is a proposed definition for a noun phrase:

Noun phrase → Determiner + Noun + Number

The noun itself is a word class which is both large and inclusive. Two major divisions are *concrete* nouns (nouns which tell how much or how many and *abstract* nouns (nouns which represent a fact, an idea, or a problem). Concrete nouns may

---

23. Structuralists and transformationalists accept the same general definition of determiner.

be further subdivided into *mass* nouns and *count* nouns. The difference is usually stated as follows: mass nouns cannot be counted serially and do not have plurals. (*Pleasure,* however, is given in some sources as a mass noun—one usually does not count *pleasure* but she certainly can speak of *pleasures.*) *Bread* and *gold* are examples of mass nouns; *flower* and *house* are examples of count nouns. Nouns may be further classified as *animate* or *inanimate. Boy, woman,* and *dog* are examples of animate nouns; *bread* and *gold,* inanimate. Animate nouns may be classified as *human* or *nonhuman. Boy* and *woman* are examples of the former, *dog* of the latter. Sentence → Noun Phrase + Verb Phrase is the basic sentence formula:

Sentence: The dogs barked.

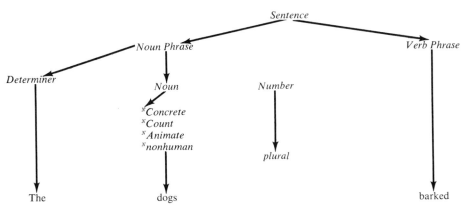

Helping Children Understand the Noun Phrase. The following exercises may be helpful in developing an understanding of the noun phrase:

A. In the following sentences, identify the noun as abstract or concrete, then further identify the concrete nouns as mass or count nouns.

1. Bill put his book on the table.
2. Mary is bringing dessert.
3. School means hard work.
4. Vacation is coming soon.
5. Birds flew overhead.

What "tests" did you use to decide whether a noun is concrete or abstract?

B. Illustrate the preceding sentences by making a tree graph.

The Verb Phrase

The verb phrase is perhaps most easily and clearly understood if the following sentences are noted.

1. The girl walks slowly.
2. The girl is walking slowly.
3. The boy has walked slowly.

4. The boy will walk slowly.
5. The girl has been walking slowly.
6. The girl may be walking slowly.
7. The boy could have walked slowly.
8. The boy must have been walking slowly.

The reader's attention is directed particularly to the variety and flexibility of material which can appear within verb phrases. It may be simply characterized as containing an auxiliary and a main verb. *Auxiliary* is here defined or interpreted as including tense—past and present. Other tenses are handled, in transformational grammar, as combinations of auxiliary parts. In the preceding numbered sentences, *will, must,* and so forth, are called *modals* and operate as very important auxiliaries. In changing from present to perfect, *have* is inserted between the present and the main verb. In some cases, the verb form becomes the past participle (He goes—He has gone—He will have gone).

The "main verb" may be indicated as follows:

Main Verb:

be + predicate

linking verb + predicate

mid-verb and noun phrase

transitive verb and noun phrase

intransitive verb

Be is the smallest class, the class with only one member (remember, however, that *is, was, are* and so forth, are included in this class, not just the verb *be* in that form only).

The term *predicate* here includes the predicate noun, the predicate adjective, and the predicate adverb, which follow *be,* and the linking verb. Examples of linking verbs: *remain, stay, become, fall, look, taste,* and *feel.*

The transitive and intransitive verbs can be modified by a *how* adverb. The transitive verb requires a noun phrase as an object and can be put in passive voice. The mid-verb, as might be assumed, stands somewhere in the middle of these two; a noun phrase is required, but it cannot be made passive or modified. Examples of these verb classifications are as follows:

Transitive verbs: *see, kick, hit, throw*
Intransitive verbs: *walk, go, run, stand, be*
Mid-verbs: *lack, have, weigh, cost*

Some attention to predicates seems to be in order at this point. The predicate can assume any of the following forms: the noun phrase (already discussed in the preceding section), the adjective (The woman grew *old*), and the locative (Put the ball *here*). The "manner" adverbial classification answers the "how" questions raised by a noun phrase and verb phrase (The boy ran *swiftly*). The sentence "The children have eaten the candy" would be tree diagrammed as follows:

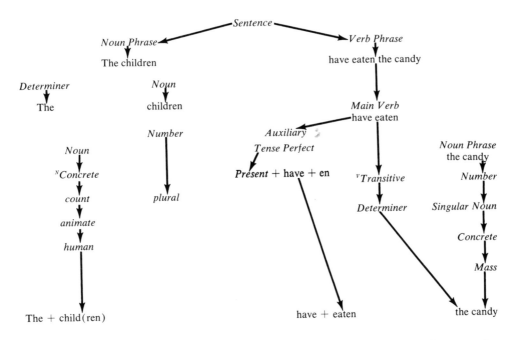

Helping Children Understand the Verb Phrase. The following exercises may be helpful in developing some understanding of the verb phrase:

A. Classify the following verbs under appropriate headings: (Linking, Intransitive; and Transitive) *remain, see, kick, hit, throw, walk, slay, run.*

B. List some other locative adverbs in addition to the following: *inside, here, there.*

C. List some other manner adverbs in addition to the following: *slowly, swiftly, gently.*

D. In the sentence "Jeff may wash the car," *wash* is the verb. *May* belongs to a small class of words called modals. Other modals are *will, shall, can,* and *must.* Try each of these modals in the blank left in this sentence. Mary _____ drive the car.

E. Any verb phrase contains a verb or a form of *to be.* There are five forms of *be* (not including *be, been,* and *being*). What are they?

It is hoped that the reader has some concept of the kernel sentences at this point. Space does not permit further explanation, nor will there be opportunity to examine more than one simple "transform" of a kernel sentence. The "question" transform is a useful one. Consider the following pairs of statements:

The girl is pretty.
Is the girl pretty?

In order to form a yes or no question, all that must be done is to move the verb and whatever constituent happens to be with it to the beginning of the sentence.

> The girl is pretty.
> Is the girl pretty?

In changing "The man ate his dinner" to "Did the man eat his dinner?" the problem is a bit more complex. The verb *do* assumes the initial position, and the original verb shifts back to its base form.

> ate—Did . . . eat. . . .

Transformational grammar becomes much too complex, from this point on, to be treated adequately in a book with the limited scope of this one. It is hoped that, at least, the reader sees the similarities and the contrasts between structural and transformational grammar. Moreover, it is hoped that the reader recognizes that there is much disciplined study behind linguists' recommendations and that just as progress has caused us to look at newer ways of teaching science and mathematics in the elementary school, it is probably most desirable to subject our English programs to close scrutiny and to make some needed changes.

Case Grammar

A third, and some would say superior, approach to linguistic analysis has recently been proposed. Several labels have been applied to this approach, and there are significant differences of opinion among the linguists who belong to this "school." One important belief held in common is that language study cannot be divorced from semantics, the study of meaning; another is that both structuralists and transformationalists take an atomistic view of language, ignoring the whole or form of the parts (the major "part" being the sound unit or phoneme for the structuralist, the combination of these sound units into sentences for the transformationalist). Wallace Chafe writes:

> It may be useful to compare this view of language with two other views which, in sequence, have dominated thinking about language in the United States since the 1920's. The earlier view, which prevailed until the late 1950's, was that which has often come under the heading of structuralism. The view which replaced it to a large extent, and is still dominant, goes under such names as transformational or generative transformational theory. I shall refer to it here as syntacticism for reasons that will become apparent. Both of these views were founded on a basic distrust of semantic data, a distrust which led inevitably to an overemphasis on the phonetic side of language.[24]

Chafe places responsibility for this overemphasis on two factors: a distrust of any data which are not concretely observable; and the relative ease with which phonetic data could be observed. The description of a sentence as consisting of a noun phrase and a verb phrase says too little about the relationship between these two

---

24. Chafe, *Meaning and the Structure of Language*, p. 60.

elements, in the opinion of most semanticists or "case grammarians." Fillmore contends that "the sentence in its basic structure consists of a verb and one or more noun phrases, each associated with the verb in a particular case relationship."[25] Chafe is in essential agreement. He writes: "My assumption will be that the total human conceptual universe is dichotomized initially into two major areas. One, the area of the verb, embraces state conditions, qualities and events, the other, the area of the noun, embraces "things" (both physical objects and reified abstractions). Of these two, the verb will be assumed to be central and the noun peripheral."[26]

Sentences as They Are Described
in Case Grammars

Fillmore *describes* a sentence as Sentence → Modality + Proposition (S → M + P). The term *proposition* refers to a tenseless set of relationships involving nouns and verbs; the term *modality* refers to such factors as tense, mood, and negative. While he admits that his list may not be exhaustive, he suggests the following as cases that appear to be needed:

Agentive (A), the case of the typically animate perceived instigator of the action.

Instrumental (I), the case of the inanimate force or object causally involved in the action or state identified by the verb.

Dative (D), the case of the animate being affected by the state or action identified by the verb.

Factitive (F), the case of the object or being resulting from the action or state identified by the verb, or understood as a part of the meaning of the verb.

Locative (L), the case which identifies the location or spatial orientation of the state or action identified by the verb.

Objective (O), the semantically most neutral case, the case of anything representable by a noun whose role in the action or state identified by the verb is identified by the semantic interpretation of the verb itself; conceivably the concept should be limited to things which are identified by the verb. The term is not to be confused with the notion of direct object, nor with the name of the surface case synonymous with accusative.[27]

Brown adds to this list:

Patient—someone or something either in a given state or suffering a change of state.

Beneficiary—someone who profits from a state in process including possession.

Experiencer—someone having a given experience or mental disposition.

Complement—the verb names an action that brings something into existence. The complement, on a more or less specific level, completes the verb.[28]

25. Charles Fillmore "The Case for Case," in *Universals in Linguistic Theory,* ed. Emmon Bach and Robert Harms,(New York: Holt, Rinehart & Winston, 1968), p. 21.
26. Chafe, *Meaning and the Structure of Language,* p. 96.
27. Fillmore, "The Case for Case," p. 25.
28. Roger Brown, *A First Language* (Cambridge, Mass.: Harvard University Press, 1970), p. 8.

Admitting that his list may also be incomplete, Brown concludes:

> How finally roles ought to be defined is unsettled; ultimately each role is a little different depending on the verb involved. That truth does not obscure the fact that a limited set of general roles such as those set down . . . seems to occur in all languages.[29]

Why so much emphasis on the verb? First, because verbs are present in all languages, except in a few marginal utterances (Oh! Ouch!, and so forth). Second, because it is the verb that determines what the rest of the sentence will be like. Noam Chomsky and other transformational-generative grammarians take the opposite position, but Chafe contends:

> There seems no need for some independent symbols as the starting point for the generation of sentences; the verb is all the starting point we need. What we may call for convenience a sentence is either a verb alone, a verb accompanied by one or more nouns, or a configuration of this kind to which one or more coordinate or subordinate verbs has been added.[30]

Helping Children Understand Case Grammar. The issues related to memorizing parts of speech, sentence patterns, or contrasts between count and mass nouns are just as significant in dealing with instructional techniques designed to help pupils understand case grammar as they are when dealing with structural and/or transformational grammar. *Assuming* the desirability of knowing the labels and the relationships implied by the labels, the following sentences may be useful as examples or might typify those developed by children, on the basis of which the teacher identifies the appropriate labels. Both Brown's and Fillmore's terms are used, where appropriate.

Agent (Agentive)   *Bob* ran all the way home.
Instrument (Instrumental)   Tim won the game with a *basket* in the final seconds.
Beneficiary   *Mary Ann* earned a good grade.
Experiencer   *Susan* is feeling very depressed.
Patient   *His* cold is much worse today.
Dative   *Ellen* was sure she would be elected class president.
Factitive   His father's death changed *Robert's career plans.*
Location (Locative)   She's gone to *school.*
Complement   They played *bridge.*
Objective   He totaled his *car.*

The differences between Instrument, Beneficiary, Experiencer, and Patient are primarily differences in degree and animation (Instrument is usually inanimate). The concept is not a difficult one, and the differences may or may not be a justification for memorizing all four labels. As the writer reviewed the more recent material,

---

29. Ibid., p. 11.
30. Chafe, *Meaning and the Structure of Language,* p. 98.

she noted that lists were becoming increasingly lengthy, and thus less appropriate for elementary classroom use. The position has been taken, with reference to the other grammars discussed, that the "inductive" or "discovery" approach is probably of more lasting value than a more didactic method. This is true of case grammar as well. If case grammar is to be treated seriously, some labels will probably have to be learned; Agent, Instrument, and Location are fairly easy to understand. Using selections from tradebooks and from their own writing, children might identify these terms *and,* more importantly, discuss the role of the verb and its relationship to the identified role. There might also be value in discussing "mode"; question (*What* did you say?); imperative (*Come* here!). This can't be any more difficult than learning the rewrite rules necessary for changing a statement to a question.

Case grammars, or generative semantics, in the mid 1970s, are about where transformational grammar was approximately ten or fifteen years ago. They are still in the developmental stages, and classroom applications have yet to be clarified. Linguistic analyses based upon relationships among or between sentence parts appear to be rational, if not totally susceptible to empirical analysis. It will be most interesting to see what adjustments transformational grammarians make in their positions, if any. There is, as yet, no successful refutation of the position that the complete grammar of the English language has not yet been written and probably never will be.

Acquisition of Syntax

Although one still reads statements suggesting that language development is relatively complete before age six, there is abundant evidence, briefly reviewed in chapter 1, that this is not the case in phonology, morphology, or syntax. The results of Carol Chomsky's research clearly indicate that development in the area of syntax continues through age ten, the highest age level she studied. Forty children between the ages of five and ten participated in individual testing sessions designed to determine their understanding of four syntactic structures:

Structure	*Difficulty*
1. John is easy to see.	1. subject of sentence subject of see
2. John promised Bill to go.	2. subject of go
3. John asked Bill what to do.	3. subject of do
4. He knew that John was going to win the race.	4. reference of he

There was considerable variation, and structures one, two, and three were strongly influenced by individual rates of development. All nine year olds knew structures one and two, but few below the age of 5.6 knew them. By age 5.6, structure four had been acquired, but some ten year olds still had trouble with structure three.

Chomsky concludes:

The significance of these results lies in the surprisingly late acquisition of syntactic structures that they reveal and the differences that they bring to light concerning the nature of the linguistic processes studied. Contrary to the commonly held view that a child has mastered the structures of his native language by the time he reaches the age of 6, we find that active syntactic acquisition is taking place up to the age of 9 and perhaps even beyond. Second, our observations regarding *order* and *rate* of acquisition for related structures in different children are in agreement with the findings of investigators who have worked with younger children. By tracing the child's orderly progress in the acquisition of a segment of his language, we are able to observe, for a set of related structures, considerable variation in rate of acquisition in different children together with a shared order of acquisition. Quite simply, although we cannot say just when a child will acquire the structures in question, we can offer a reliable judgement about the relative order in which we will acquire them.[31]

Chomsky's study is highly significant for teachers, suggesting the need to expect and facilitate syntactic growth throughout the entire elementary school period. The term *facilitate* can be interpreted in a number of ways, but since language development and cognitive development are so closely related, instructional procedures and materials (questioning and discussion techniques, for example) designed to promote development in one area should promote growth in the other. The extent to which a "Language Acquisition Device" (LAD), essentially biological in nature, controls syntactic growth is an issue beyond the scope of this text. It seems increasingly clear that development in this, as in other facets of language, is orderly and sequential, perhaps even invariant. Nevertheless, few would suggest that this means that parents, siblings, peers, even teachers, have no impact at all on language development. The LAD, if such exists, sets the outer limits, and may determine the rate, of language acquisition and development, but many, many physical, emotional, and social factors combine to assist, or deter, this process.

Kellogg Hunt conducted two studies of significance to those interested in the development of syntactic maturity. He was credited with developing the concept of the T unit, or minimal terminable unit, one main clause plus all the subordinate clauses attached to it. It was Hunt's contention that this provided a better index of syntactic maturity than sentence length. Significant changes were found in number of T units as the writing of fourth, eighth, and twelfth graders (nine, of average IQ, at each grade level, enrolled in a university laboratory school) was analyzed and compared with the writing of superior adults:

Although the average child in the fourth grade produces virtually all the grammatical structures ever described in a course in school grammar, he does not produce as many at the same time—as many inside each other, or on top of each other—as older students do. He does subordinate some clauses to others, but not as many. He does reduce some coordinated clauses to coordinations inside a single clause, but not

---

31. Carol Chomsky, *The Acquisition of Syntax in Children From Five to Ten* (Cambridge, Mass.: M.I.T. Press, 1969), pp. 120–21.

enough. He does put several clauses into a t unit, but not as many as older students do. He does write some complicated nominals, but his are never as highly complicated. It is what the older student does *in extremis* that especially distinguishes him.[32]

In terms of curricular implications, Hunt notes that complicated grammatical structures are usually taught, if at all, to older pupils:

> Against such motivation this study provides strong evidence. The structures studied here are at least as complex as those studied in most school grammar courses. Indeed they are probably more complex than those taught in most college courses called 'advanced grammar'. Yet they are virtually all used by fourth graders and are used often enough and successfully enough to indicate that fourth graders command them. This study provides no justification for not going straight through a description of grammatical structures once such a course is begun.[33]

O'Donnell, Griffin, and Norris analyzed the oral and written language of elementary school pupils; oral samples were obtained from pupils in kindergarten and first, second, third, fifth, and seventh grades (about 30 at each level); writing samples were obtained from third, fifth, and seventh graders. Findings indicated that T unit length increased with age, in both oral and written discourse. Apparently, as they matured, children learned to use a larger and larger number of sentence-combining transformations per main clause, both in speech and writing.[34]

Hunt's second study involved more pupils (more than a thousand), more grade levels, (fourth, sixth, eighth, tenth, and twelfth), and probably a more typical population, since these pupils were enrolled in the public schools of Tallahassee, Florida. Students and two groups of adults were asked to rewrite, "in a better way," a passage about aluminum that was deliberately short and choppy in terms of sentence structure. The primary difference between the assigned tasks in the first and second studies Hunt directed was that in the second task, constraints were applied through this paragraph which all writers were instructed to rewrite. In the first study, subjects were permitted to write without such topic constraints. The conclusions reached on the basis of the findings of this study were quite similar to those based on the findings of the first study. Older writers demonstrated a much greater repertoire of syntactic resources to draw upon than younger and took advantage of more opportunities for consolidating sentences. Further, some transformations seemed to indicate greater syntactic maturity than others. That is, a few constructions used by younger writers were replaced by more sophisticated constructions in the writing of older subjects.

In view of the controversy regarding the value of instruction in grammar in the elementary school, Hunt's recommendations are interesting and in direct contradiction to those of James Moffett. Hunt writes:

---

32. Kellogg Hunt, *Grammatical Structures Written at Three Grade Levels* (Champaign, Ill.: National Council of Teachers of English, 1965), p. 156.

33. Ibid., p. 155.

34. Roy O'Donnell, W. C. Griffin, and R. C. Norris, *Syntax of Kindergarten and Elementary School Children: A Transformational Analysis* (Champaign, Ill.: National Council of Teachers of English, 1967).

At least two curricula designed to increase sentence embedding have been tried out for a year and have been tested to see whether they produce more than the usual amount of growth in the students' writing. One study (Mellon, 1967) was made in the seventh grade; one (Miller and Ney, 1968) was made in fourth. Both report that the experimental group showed significantly more growth than a comparable control group, and neither experimenter observed any deleterious effects.

a) In view of these successful first attempts it seems advisable that a variety of curricula be designed to facilitate syntactic maturity.

b) It seems advisable that a sequential curriculum on syntactic maturity covering many grades, perhaps all, should be undertaken.

c) It seems advisable that teachers of writing at all levels should be trained in at least the rudiments of transformational theory. Though, like any other scientific theory, this one is neither complete, definitive, nor static, it does offer useful insights to the teacher.[35]

Grammar in the Elementary Classroom

Some attention must be given to Moffett's position on instruction in grammar in the elementary school, which, as noted, is in sharp contrast to Hunt's position. He sees little value in it, at this level, and writes:

Probably no other area of the language arts except beginning reading is so bedev-illed with semantic confusion as grammar teaching. What kind of knowledge of grammar does one mean—a working knowledge or a conceptual grasp of gram-matical generalizations? What kind of grammar—prescriptive or descriptive, a body of rules for correct usage in the standard dialect, or a systematic schematization of syntactic relations? If descriptive, a classificatory, structural or generative grammar? What kind of instruction—identifying parts of speech, filling in blanks with the correct linguistic form, parsing and diagramming sentence examples, making up sentences on a grammatical paradigm or pattern, memorizing concepts and codifica-tions about the operations of syntax? And finally, improvement in what aspect of writing—the "mechanics" of punctuation and capitalization, the correction of 'me and him went to town', the expansion of the syntactic repertory in the direction of elaboration and diversification of sentence constructions, or the development of judgment in sentence construction as measured by communicative effectiveness and rhetorical advantage?[36]

Moffett's conclusion regarding the value of studying grammar in the elementary school is worth serious consideration:

Rational inquiry into language must not be allowed at its very outset to fall prey, like composition, to the overblown influence of sentence analysis.[37]

---

35. Kellogg Hunt, *Syntactic Maturity in School Children and Adults* (Chicago: University of Chicago Press, 1970), p. 60.
36. James Moffett, *Teaching the Universe of Discourse* (Boston: Houghton Mifflin Co., 1968), pp. 155–56.
37. Ibid., p. 186.

There is obvious merit to Moffett's strong position, and whether or not one agrees with it—most textbook publishers and English teachers probably don't, his warning about emphasizing sentence analysis to the detriment of "style" or generally effective writing should be heeded. The issue of sentence combining and expansion provides a good case in point. Obviously, young writers can be taught rules for combining and embedding,[38, 39, 40] and can be forced to display this knowledge or ability in compositions. Does this necessarily guarantee a *better* composition (oral or written)? Probably not. Few would contend that longer, more involved sentences are better sentences—this can hardly be the basis for a reader's relative preference for Hemingway or Faulkner.

However, in spite of the fact that instruction in grammar *cannot* be justified on the basis of improvement in pupils' writing or speaking, it will probably continue to occupy a prominent role in most language programs, and, thus, grammar deserves and has received major consideration in this book.

The "functional" aspect of mathematics is receiving much less emphasis than it did only a few years ago. The "new math" programs emphasize the *structure* of mathematics—and this is precisely the position of many linguists; it is the *structure* of language which should receive instructional emphasis. They consider it a bonus if a child's speech and composition improve as a result of our language programs, but the primary goal is to develop a thorough understanding of American English and how it operates.

The elementary or middle school teacher may or may not find the use of a textbook series essential for purposes of articulation and comprehensiveness in language arts programs. Whatever the decision regarding a textbook, the tape recorder, chalkboard, and pupils' writing may well prove to be a teacher's most useful teaching tools. If the decision is made to include instruction in grammar, it should *not* mean discontinuance of strong emphasis on learning about language by *using* it.

It is difficult to overemphasize the value of the literature program in sensitizing children to a writer's use of language. Two short passages written by the same writer might be compared, and so can the treatments of similar topics by different authors. The list of books *about* language included in the references at the end of chapter 1 should also be of assistance in developing this "syntactic sensitivity."

By the time a child leaves the elementary school, she should be conscious of the language patterns she uses for different situations. Because her teachers understand the nature of standard English, so will she. She should be aware of the relationship between speech sounds and writing. In addition to expanding her understanding of the phonology of her language, she will be expanding her knowledge of syntax, the arrangement of words in sentences and paragraphs. Hopefully, the increasing depth of understanding which the child brings to all of her classroom experiences with

38. Donald Bateman and Frank Zidonis, *The Effect of a Study of Transformational Grammar on the Writing of Ninth and Tenth Graders* (Champaign, Ill.: The National Council of Teachers of English, 1966).

39. John Mellon, "Transformational Sentence-Combining, A Method of Enhancing the Development of Syntactic Fluency in English Composition," Harvard University, Project 5-8418, Cooperative Research Bureau, United States Office of Education.

40. Hunt, *Grammatical Structures Written at Three Grade Levels.*

speaking and writing (panel discussions, reports, planning sessions) will result in increasing effectiveness with these tools. It may be true, as some linguists say, that language is important enough to study for its inherent values, and, thus, it really shouldn't matter whether language study results in improved functional operation with language or not.

Evaluation of Children's Programs in Grammar and Usage

There is little to say about evaluating in this area which has not already been said about evaluating spelling and reading, but perhaps some specific corollaries can be noted. Most of the usual standardized achievement tests are not "keyed" to either structural or transformational grammar (at this time) and may be inappropriate. Those responsible for selecting tests should recognize the possible discrepancy between what is taught and what is tested.

Teacher-made tests are a valuable tool for assessing children's growth in understanding the grammar of their language. Some in-service work would be of tremendous value in helping teachers gain needed sophistication in test construction.

Pursuing the tenuous line already taken, it does not seem unwise to look carefully at children's writing for evidence of growth in the use of a variety of patterns. Children themselves should develop the ability to analyze their own writing and an awareness of their strengths and weaknesses.

Summary

There was a temptation in writing such a far-ranging chapter as this one to deal with structural grammar *or* transformational grammar *or* case grammar. The controversy which surrounds these approaches is discussed earlier in this book. Because each approach, particularly the latter two, has considerable support, it was decided to include all three. It is hoped that the reader will compare these grammars, note their similarities and differences with respect to traditional grammar, and judge for herself which is more "teachable" and which would result in better understanding and appreciation of our language. Each appears to have merit, and, especially if past achievement records are considered, each promises to be at least as productive (if not more so) than the traditional grammars so deeply entrenched in our schools. The issue of whether or not teaching specific elements of grammar to elementary school pupils is of value was raised. If the application of knowledge regarding sentence embedding and other combining techniques does indeed produce more sophisticated (mature?) writing, does this necessarily mean that the writing is *better?* The answer to this question must rest on philosophical bases, difficult to resolve through typical scientific-experimental strategies.

It is surely time for a reexamination in the area of language study. Just as mathematics programs and science programs in elementary schools have, in general, benefited from renewed curricular emphasis and the contribution of mathematicians and scientists (as well as educators), so can the linguist help in setting guidelines and providing the scientific basis for new language programs. Linguists are not elementary teachers, and it must be elementary teachers, supervisors, and administrators who determine the curricular implications and applications of linguists' recommendations.

Selected References

Allen, Harold, ed. "English Linguistics Today" and "Linguistics and Usage." In *Readings in Applied English Linguistics*. New York: Appleton-Century-Crofts, 1964.

Anderson, Paul. *Language Skills in Elementary Education,* chapter 8. New York: MacMillan Co., 1972.

Borgh, Enola. *Grammatical Patterns and Composition*. Oshkosh: Wisconsin Council of Teachers of English, 1963.

Brown, Roger. *A First Language: The Early Stages*. Cambridge, Mass.: Harvard University Press, 1973.

————, and Ursula Bellugi. "Three Processes in the Child's Acquisition of Syntax." *Harvard Educational Review* 34 (1964): 133–51.

Chomsky, Carol. *The Acquisition of Syntax in Children from Five to Ten*. Cambridge, Mass.: M.I.T. Press, 1969.

Chomsky, Noam. *Reflections on Language*. New York: Pantheon Books, 1975.

Crystal, David. *Linguistics*. Harmondsworth, Middlesex, England: Penguin Books, 1971.

Cullinan, Bernice, ed. *Black Dialects and Reading*. Urbana, Ill.: National Council of Teachers of English, 1974.

DeLancey, Robert. *Linguistics and Teaching*. Rochester: New York State English Council, 1965.

Fasold, Ralph, and Roger Shuy, eds. *Teaching Standard English in the Inner City*. Washington, D.C.: Center for Applied Linguistics, 1970.

Fillmore, Charles. "The Case for Case." In *Universals in Linguistics Theory*, edited by Emmon Bach and Robert Harms. New York: Holt, Rinehart & Winston, 1968.

Francis, W. Nelson. *The Structure of American English*, chapters 5, 6, 7. New York: Ronald Press Co., 1958.

Gleason, Henry, Jr. *Linguistics and English Grammar*. New York: Holt, Rinehart & Winston, 1965.

Greene, Judith. *Psycholinguistics: Chomsky and Psychology*. Harmondsworth, Middlesex, England: Penguin Books, 1972.

Hunt, Kellogg. *Grammatical Structures Written at Three Grade Levels*. Champaign, Ill.: The National Council of Teachers of English, 1965.

————. *Syntactic Maturity in School Children and Adults*. Chicago: University of Chicago Press, 1970.

Ives, Sumner. "Some Notes on Syntax and Meaning." *The Reading Teacher* 18 (1964): 179–83.

Joos, Martin. "Language and the School Child." *Harvard Educational Review* 34 (1964): 203–10.

"Language Explorations for the Elementary Grades," "Poetry in the Elementary Grades," and "Curriculum Guides, Grades 1-6." In *A Curriculum for English.* Lincoln: University of Nebraska Press, 1966.

Mellon, John. *A Grammar for English Sentences, Book One: Basic Sentence Types and Their Simple Transforms.* Culver, Ind.: Culver Military Academy, 1964.

Menyuk, Paula. *Sentences Children Use.* Cambridge, Mass.: M.I.T. Press, 1969.

Moffett, James. *Teaching the Universe of Discourse.* Boston: Houghton Mifflin Co., 1968.

Newsome, Verna. *Structural Grammar in the Classroom.* (Oshkosh: Wisconsin Council of Teachers of English, 1962.

Roberts. Paul. *English Sentences.* New York: Harcourt Brace Jovanovich, 1962.

———. *English Syntax.* New York: Harcourt Brace Jovanovich, 1964.

Robinson, Ian. *The New Grammarians' Funeral.* Cambridge: At the University Press, 1975.

Stageburg, Norman. *An Introductory English Grammar.* New York: Holt, Rinehart & Winston, 1965.

Staiger, Ralph. "Language Arts Research, 1964." *Elementary English* 42 (1965): 433–45.

Materials for Children

Several valuable teaching aids have already been suggested. They are restated here because of their significance.

a. tape recordings of discussions, reports, and so forth, analyzed for sentence structure as well as for content
b. selected examples from children's literature, read or listened to for structure and organization as well as content
c. selected examples of children's written work—reports, stories, poems—analyzed for purposes of structure

It seems unwise to list textbook series; nearly all the published materials represent a rather fixed position on the continuum from no treatment of grammar to a rather thorough treatment, sequentially organized, of transformational grammar. At this time, the writer knows of no texts based on case grammar, but some may be produced in the near future. Once teachers have determined *how much* grammar to teach, it should not be difficult to find an appropriate textbook series, particularly if the grammar selected is structural or transformational.

Postscript

This book represents an effort to find answers to one of the most important questions an educator might (should?) ask: Why study language? Noam Chomsky's excellent answer to that question follows:

> Why study language? There are many possible answers, and by focusing on some I do not, of course, mean to disparage others, or question their legitimacy. One may, for example, be fascinated by the elements of language in themselves and want to discover their order and arrangement, their origin in history or in the individual, or the way in which they are used in thought, in science or in art, or in normal social interchange. One reason for studying language—and for me personally the most compelling reason—is that it is tempting to regard language, in the traditional phase, as "a mirror of mind." I do not mean by this simply that the concepts expressed and distinctions developed in normal language use give us insight into the patterns of thought and the world of "common sense" constructed by the human mind. More intriguing, to me at least, is the possibility that by studying language we may discover abstract principles that govern its structure and use, principles that are universal by biological necessity and not mere historical accident, that derive from mental characteristics of the species. A human language is a system of remarkable complexity. To come to know a human language would be an extraordinary intellectual achievement for a creature not specifically designed to accomplish this task. A normal child acquires this knowledge on relatively slight exposure and without specific training. He can then quite effortlessly make use of an intricate structure of

specific rules and guiding principles to convey his thoughts and feelings to others, arousing in them word ideas and subtle perceptions and judgments. For the conscious mind, not specifically designed for the purpose, it remains a distant goal to comprehend what the child has done intuitively and with minimal effort. Thus, language is a mirror of mind in a deep and significant sense. It is a product of human intelligence, created anew in each individual by operations that lie far beyond the reach of will or consciousness.[1]

There can hardly be a search, or a quest, of more significance for a teacher than that identified by Noam Chomsky. And even though the search may be only partly successful, the question answered in only a limited sense, the teacher is almost certain to profit from the results of the observations, the reading, and the other data gathering which are essential to guiding children's language learning and, thus, facilitating their cognitive functioning.

---

1. From *Reflections on Language* by Noam Chomsky. Copyright © 1975 by Random House, Pantheon Books. (pp. 3–4.)

Glossary

It is almost unnecessary to state that many linguists would question a number of the following attempts at defining some of the terminology used in this text and encountered in most of the linguistically oriented material which the classroom teacher may read. The definitions included have been selected or developed on the basis of their practical applicability to aspects of the language arts curriculum in the elementary school, and the major concern has been for interpreting linguistic terminology for the teacher, rather than developing definitions which would be scientifically accurate and acceptable to most, if not all, linguists. Several definitions have been included for some terms, and where definitions have been developed by linguists, full credit has been given to the source.

Affix. A bound morpheme which occurs before or behind a base; i.e., un_____,
_____ing. (It follows, then, that a *prefix* is an affix which occurs *before* a base,
un_____; and a *suffix* is an affix which occurs *following* a base, _____*ing*.)

Allomorph. An allomorph bears the same relationship to a morpheme as an allophone
bears to a phoneme; an allomorph is a variation of a morpheme. The words *a* and
an are allomorphs of one morpheme, *a.* They have the same meaning; *a* is used
before consonants, *an* before vowels.

Allophone. All the members of one phoneme class; they are phonetically similar to other
members of the phoneme class to which they belong and do *not* indicate contrasts in
meaning. The [t¹] at the end of *mint* and the [t] at the end of *seat* are allophones of
the phoneme /t/. Brackets are typically used to indicate allophones, slanted lines to
indicate phonemes.

Determiner. A word preceding a noun and signaling that a noun is to follow. Determiners may also be used in places of nouns, as noun substitutes.

Dialect. A variation of a language sufficiently different to be considered a separate entity, but not different enough to be classed as a separate language. These differences occur in vocabulary and pronunciation, and to a limited extent, in grammatical construction. Dialects generally do *not* affect the writing system of a language, and evidence that it interferes with reading achievement is lacking.

Digraph. Two successive letters represent a single sound, as *ea* in *bread,* or two letters whose value is not the sum of the value possessed by each, as *ch* in *chair.* A digraph has also been defined as a group of two successive letters (Webster's Seventh New Collegiate Dictionary).

Diphthong. A combination of two vowel sounds, beginning with one sound, gliding to another, as in *oil* or *toy.*

Grapheme. The written representation of the sounds of a language; a letter or letters which represent(s) a phoneme. Spelling, or orthography, is the writing of graphemes in proper order to form morphemes.

Homographs. The written representation of words which appear to be similar in their orthography but have different meanings and different pronunciations, i.e., *record:* \ri-'kȯrd\ *or* \'rek-ərd\; *row:* \'rō\ *or* \'raủ\.

Homophones. Groups of words in American English which sound alike but have different meanings and, usually, different spellings as well: *to, two, too; meet, meat; sea, see.*

Juncture. Some structural linguists have identified four significant types of juncture (or pause). One is *internal* or open, and the others are terminal; the latter may be written as follows:

Plus juncture: + (a + name – an + aim)
Single bar juncture: /My friend/Jack/isn't here
Double bar juncture: //one//two//three//four
Double cross juncture: #one #two# three# four#

Single bar juncture, where speech is terminated abruptly and remains on a level pitch . . . is sometimes, but quite rarely, associated with punctuation.[1] In double bar juncture (a rising, terminal juncture) the voice is less sharply cut off, and there is a rise in pitch before the pause; this rise is part of the juncture, which is, therefore, something more than just a pause . . . the double cross juncture (a falling, terminal juncture) is associated with a drop in pitch and a fading off or trailing away of the voice into silence. This can be discerned at the end of most statement utterances in American English, and is typically associated in written English with some form of end punctuation.[2]

Linguist. A scholar (scientist) whose training is in the field of human languages. The types of linguists may be characterized as follows:

Descriptive linguist: A scientist whose major interest is recording and describing significant features of the languages of the world.

Historical linguist: A scientist whose major interest is tracing (1) the origins of

---

1. That is, the comma, colon, or semicolon represents a "break" in the idea being communicated.

2. Robert DeLancey, *Linguistics and Teaching* (Rochester, New York: Council of Teachers of English, 1965), p. 20.

various types of sentence patterns and (2) the development of dialects and languages.[3]

   Psycholinguist: A scholar whose interests include cognitive and linguistic development and the relationship between the two.

   Sociolinguist: A scholar whose professional concerns include the impact of society (culture?) upon language, and vice versa.

Linguistics. The scientific study of human languages.[4] The following are often considered major branches of the science:

   Phonology: The scientific study of the sounds of language.

   Etymology: The scientific study of the origins and derivations of words.

Morpheme. The smallest meaning-bearing units of a language, consisting of certain phonemes or combinations of phonemes. Also "a word, or part of a word, that bears meaning; indivisible into smaller parts without violation of its meaning or meaningless remainders."[5]

Noun. The definition of parts of speech is typically avoided by linguists. "A noun is the name of a person, place, or thing . . ." is particularly unacceptable to linguists because it is functional rather than structural, and because it is inadequate; it does not "cover" enough cases. If a definition is provided, the following is preferred: "Nouns are identified as nouns by two aspects of form, their inflectional morphemes are the noun possessives, and the noun plural . . . their derivational morphemes. Nouns may also be formed by adding noun-forming suffixes to adjectives, verbs, etc. . . ."[6]

Pitch. The tonal quality in speech which becomes part of the signaling system in American English. There is general agreement among linguists in the identification of four levels of pitch, as follows:

   4: extra high (surprise, shock, fear, and so forth)

   3: high

   2: normal

   1: low

The role of pitch as a meaning-bearing agent might be illustrated as follows:

   "[2]I'm [3]Going [1]Home." (In this message, it is the fact that I'm going home rather than somewhere else which is important.)

   "[3]I'm [2]Going [1]Home." (In this message, it is the fact that *I* am going home, whether anyone else does or not, which has significance.)

Pitch is almost invariably used in combination with stress to fully convey and understand a speaker's message.

Sentence. See the relatively complete discussion of varying points of view on this term in chapter 4.

---

   3. W. Nelson Francis, in *The Structure of American English* (New York: Ronald Press, 1958) states that the terms *diachronic and synchronic* are more acceptable. He writes that synchronic refers to "dealing with a state of affairs at a given point of time" (p. 21). Thus it is analogous to descriptive linguists. Diachronic refers to "dealing with changes that occur in time" (p. 21) and it might be compared with the less accurate term, *historical linguistics.* This difference in terminology is probably of more interest than significance to the classroom teacher.

   4. Ian Robinson is sharply critical of this concept. His entire book, (see Selected References, chapter 4) is a denial of the scientific base of linguistics.

   5. Norman Stageburg, *An Introduction to English Grammar* (Holt, Rinehart & Winston, 1965), p. 85.

   6. Ibid., p. 192.

Stress. The degree of prominence a syllable has. Some linguists identify three levels of stress; others, four. When four levels of stress are identified they are usually classified as follows:

Primary stress: indicated by ′
Secondary stress: indicated by ^
Tertiary stress: indicated by `
Weak stress: the symbol ˘ is accepted, but often a symbol is omitted entirely to indicate weak stress.

If three levels of stress are identified, they are classified as follows:

Primary stress: indicated by ′
Mid stress: indicated by ^
Weak stress: indicated by ˘ or symbol may be omitted.

Stress becomes an important meaning-bearing agent in speech, along with pitch, particularly in utterances such as:

	re′cord (noun)		per′mit (noun)
record		*permit*	
	re cord′ (verb)		per mit′ (verb)

Various dictionaries, including those used by elementary school pupils, will indicate stress in different ways. These differences might profitably be discussed and contrasts ard/or contradictions pointed out to children.

Superfixes. Word stress patterns which may or may not affect meaning. An example of the former: re′cord and re cord′; of the latter, de′tail and de tail′.

Suprasegmental phonemes. Pitch, stress, and juncture, or pause, which are significant (phonemic) because they influence meaning. The term *suprasegmental* refers to their imposition upon the segmental phonemes or significant sound units of a language.

Syntax. That phase of grammar which deals with the relationship of words in sentences and the manner in which words are put together to form sentences.

Verb. This definition must also be approached cautiously. "An action word" is both inaccurate and restrictive as a definition. Francis writes:

Verbs are a class of lexical words marked by their use of four inflections: {-s} {-ed₁} {-ed₂}[7] and {-ing}; by their appearance in verb phrases with certain auxiliaries, such as can, must, is, has, please, about (to), keep (on); by a small group of derivational affixes {en-} and {-ate}; by certain positions relative to clearly marked nouns; and occasionally by the superfix {′˘}.[8]

Word. Stageburg defines *word* as follows: "A word is a free form that cannot be divided wholly into smaller free forms."[9] It may give the reader some comfort to know that the familiar terms *simple* and *complex* are used as subclassifications of the term *word;* however, the linguists' definitions of simple and complex may not be so familiar:

Simple words consist of no more than two segmental morphemes. (Examples: *take, taken, stronger*)

Complex words are composed of two bound morphemes, one of which is a base; the other, a superfix. There may or may not be an inflectional suffix. (Examples: *televise, extract, preclude*)

---

7. {-ed₁} and {-ed₂} refer to past tense and past participle endings.
8. Francis, *The Structure of American English,* p. 267.
9. Stageburg, *Introduction to English Grammar,* p. 107. He defines a free form as any segment of speech that can be spoken alone, with meaning, in normal speech.

Index

Charles E. Merrill Publishing Company
A Bell & Howell Company
Columbus, Ohio 43216

BELL & HOWELL

8596-9